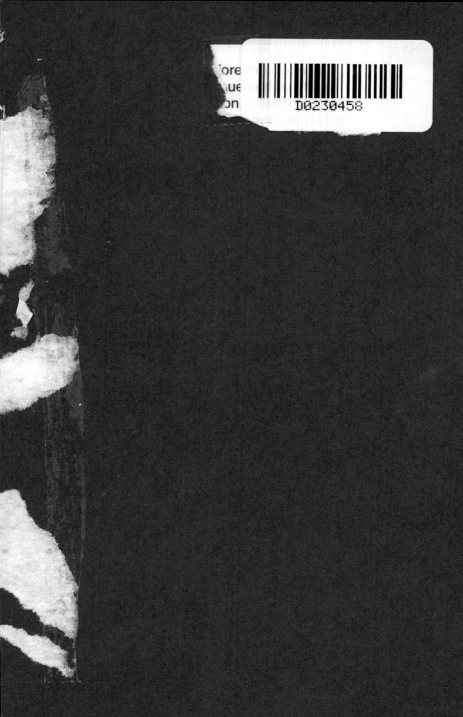

The
BRONTËSAURUS

The
BRONTËSAURUS

An A-Z of Charlotte, Emily & Anne Brontë
(& Branwell)

JOHN SUTHERLAND

ICON

Published in the UK in 2016
by Icon Books Ltd, Omnibus Business Centre,
39–41 North Road, London N7 9DP
email: info@iconbooks.com
www.iconbooks.com

Sold in the UK, Europe and Asia
by Faber & Faber Ltd, Bloomsbury House,
74–77 Great Russell Street,
London WC1B 3DA or their agents

Distributed in the UK, Europe and Asia
by Grantham Book Services, Trent Road, Grantham NG31 7XQ

Distributed in the USA
by Publishers Group West,
1700 Fourth Street, Berkeley, CA 94710

Distributed in Australia and New Zealand
by Allen & Unwin Pty Ltd,
PO Box 8500, 83 Alexander Street,
Crows Nest, NSW 2065

Distributed in South Africa
by Jonathan Ball, Office B4, The District,
41 Sir Lowry Road, Woodstock 7925

Distributed in India by Penguin Books India,
7th Floor, Infinity Tower – C, DLF Cyber City,
Gurgaon 122002, Haryana

Distributed in Canada by Publishers Group Canada,
76 Stafford Street, Unit 300,
Toronto, Ontario M6J 2S1

ISBN 978-178578-143-8

Typeset in Adobe Jenson Pro by Marie Doherty

Printed and bound in the UK by Clays Ltd, St Ives plc

ABOUT THE AUTHOR

John Sutherland is Lord Northcliffe Professor Emeritus at University College London and an eminent scholar in the field of Victorian fiction. He is the author of several books, including *The Longman Companion to Victorian Fiction* (Longman, 2009) and the bestselling popular titles *Is Heathcliff a Murderer?* (OUP, 1995) and *Can Jane Eyre Be Happy?* (OUP, 1996). His more recent works include *Lives of the Novelists: A History of Fiction in 294 Lives* (Profile, 2011) and *A Little History of Literature* (Yale, 2013).

CONTENTS

PREFACE

Like most, I suspect, who read *Wuthering Heights* early in life, the novel has smouldered in my mind ever since – rekindled by regular rereading. I remember taking the book out of the school library (an 'Everyman' edition) aged fifteen. I entered my name in the borrowing ledger.

A day or two later, a senior boy came up to me. 'How did you like it?' he asked. It was conspiratorial. He, like me, was someone who had discovered the novel. It was something to keep private, lest the teachers, who claimed they knew everything, got their pedagogic paws on it. It was secret treasure. I went on to read, over the following years, the poignantly short Brontëan oeuvre.

In my formative years, the reputation of the Brontës had to contend with the lofty anathema proclaimed by F.R. Leavis in *The Great Tradition* – a work of biblical authority in the postwar period. Leavis found no place for them in his selection of British novelists who really mattered. Charlotte's three novels had only 'interest of a minor kind', he proclaimed. *Wuthering Heights* was granted to be 'astonishing', but a 'sport': a term used by geneticists to indicate life forms outside the main evolutionary line. A freak, or deviant phenomenon. It belonged not in the great tradition of English fiction but in the Ripley's Believe It or Not! museum of literature.

The most perceptive critics of the Brontë oeuvre think differently, and more reverently, from Mrs Gaskell and Mrs Humphry Ward onward, to Daphne Du Maurier, Rebecca Fraser, Sally Shuttleworth, Margaret Smith, Lucasta Miller, Juliet Barker, Claire Harmon, Winifred Gerin, Sandra Gilbert and Susan Gerber, Gayatri Spivak, and (for me the most enlightening)

Dorothy Van Ghent. Jean Rhys (with *Wide Sargasso Sea*) and Daphne Du Maurier (with *Rebecca*) went on to elaborate Brontëan designs into second-generation Brontëan fiction, as fine as *Jane Eyre*, the work they were paying homage to. This list could be enlarged.

This fancifully entitled book is homage to the Brontës (and their most perceptive critics) in an anniversary year. It reflects, I hope, a pleasure I have had over many decades reading them, ever since that first, treasured, reading of *Wuthering Heights*.

John Sutherland

ANNE'S LAST JOURNEY

The Haworth death toll – it came as regularly as Christmas – worked against the Brontës ever mustering as a complete family. They are, nonetheless, forever gathered in one place: under the pillar over their vault in the chapel of Haworth church.

There is, however, an absentee. It's surprising, given the fact that Anne was, ostensibly, the most obedient and homebound of the four children who made it into adulthood. Anne, the baby of the family, and asthmatic, was – on grounds of physical fragility – spared the ordeal of Cowan Bridge school, the institution where TB had claimed the lives of her two eldest sisters, Maria and Elizabeth. 'Gentle' is one of the few defining epithets applied to Anne as a girl. In one of her brief spells of formal education, Anne won a 'good conduct' medal – an award which one strains to imagine decorating the juvenile breasts of Emily, Branwell or Charlotte.

But there was, her biographers argue persuasively, steel in her mix. Anne's first employment, aged eighteen, was with the Ingham family at Blake Hall, near Mirfield. The Ingham children were spoilt and malicious and she was dismissed after a year for not indulging their nastiness. It's nice to think that the Inghams lived to read themselves portrayed as the odious Bloomfields, in *Agnes Grey*.

'Gentle' and 'dutiful' as she may have been, Anne does not gild the governess's life with Jane Eyreish romanticism. She is more of Jane Fairfax's party (in Jane Austen's *Emma*) that governessing is the domestic English slave trade. Particularly stomach-turning is the depiction of young Tom Bloomfield torturing ('fettling') birds. When Agnes remonstrates, she is blandly informed that she is a servant and should mind her own business – 'by gum!'

They are lesser creation: so is she. Governesses, despite the name, govern nothing.

Anne went on to a more salubrious post with the Revd Edmund Robinson, and his wife Lydia (the destroyer of Branwell, see below, 'Branwell's Robinsoniad', page 22) at Thorp Green Hall (immortalised as Horton Lodge in *Agnes Grey*), near York. Anne was with the Robinsons for five years. Her holidays at Haworth were short. The happy, late section of *Agnes Grey* draws on her time at Thorp Green, merging finally into the happy ever after of the heroine's marriage to the ubiquitous curate in the Brontë world: something that would never, alas, happen to the author herself. (It was her sister, Charlotte, who married the ever-present curate – see below, 'Mr Charlotte Brontë', page 95.)

Particularly wonderful for Anne were the Robinson family's long summer holidays in Scarborough. The seaside resort figures in both her novels (it's near Linden-Car in *The Tenant of Wildfell Hall*). Her first publication, 'Lines Composed in a Wood on a Windy Day', is about being at Thorp Green, and dreaming about Scarborough:

> I wish I could see how the ocean is lashing
> The foam of its billows to whirlwinds of spray;
> I wish I could see how its proud waves are dashing,
> And hear the wild roar of their thunder today!

What Scarborough meant to her is expressed, ecstatically, in the penultimate chapter of *Agnes Grey*, rhapsodising about 'the sands':

> And then, the unspeakable purity and freshness of the
> air! There was just enough heat to enhance the value of

the breeze, and just enough wind to keep the whole sea in motion, to make the waves come bounding to the shore, foaming and sparkling, as if wild with glee. Nothing else was stirring – no living creature was visible besides myself. My footsteps were the first to press the firm, unbroken sands; – nothing before had trampled them since last night's flowing tide had obliterated the deepest marks of yesterday, and left it fair and even, except where the subsiding water had left behind it the traces of dimpled pools and little running streams.

Anne perhaps bathed from time to time using one of the 'machines' on the beach. But it was the air which most charmed her. Anne dreamed of setting up a school at Scarborough with her sisters, using the small inheritance their aunt Branwell left them. It happens, fictionally, in *Agnes Grey*.

Disastrously, Anne got a position for Branwell with the Robinsons in 1843. The boy, Hugh, needed a male tutor, not a governess. Branwell had a messy affair with the mistress of the house, Lydia Robinson, 'the vile seductress', as Brontë patriarch Patrick called her. She too, apparently, needed a young male.

In the last months of her life it was clear (not least to herself) that Anne was dying. The family was by now expert in the sad symptomatology of premature death. Extraordinarily, in what were her dying days – possibly hours – this most obedient of the sisters demanded, uncompromisingly, she be taken to Scarborough.

She did not want her last breath to be the toxic air of Haworth. One can see her last journey as a kind of anabasis, a wilful break for freedom, into the light – away from the morbid lazaret on the moors with its killing miasmas. No doctor would have approved the trip. But, as Emily had shown, a dying woman could defy doctors.

Anne, Charlotte and a servant left Haworth on 24 May 1849. They spent a night at York. Anne's request was that she should visit, again, York Minster (one of a number of hints that her religious views had ascended higher than those of her father and Charlotte). She was by now immobile and required a wheelchair. It was clear she was knocking at death's door. A doctor in York confirmed the sad fact. She died on 28 May, in rented lodgings, in a spot in Scarborough she particularly loved.

It would have been quite feasible to bring Anne's body back the 70 miles to Haworth (easier, in fact, to negotiate her frail body across railway changes in a coffin than it had been getting her to Scarborough in a wheelchair). But Charlotte religiously observed what were patently her sister's dying wishes, and made arrangements for burial at St Mary's Church, with a view of the bay and her beloved 'sands'. Patrick did not attend the service. He may have been distressed by his daughter's final act of separation from him.

There was, other than Anne's companions, just one (unnamed) mourner at the burial, in a temporary resting place (St Mary's, undergoing restoration, was not yet ready for her – a poignant touch in an overwhelmingly poignant death).

Charlotte returned to the grave only once, in flowering June, three years later, to visit the grave. Her reluctance is explained in the poem she wrote, bluntly entitled 'On the Death of Anne Brontë':

> There's little joy in life for me,
> And little terror in the grave;
> I've lived the parting hour to see
> Of one I would have died to save.

Mick Armitage, in the informative 'Anne Brontë – The Scarborough Connection' section of his website, records that there is no evidence that Patrick ever visited Anne's grave, despite his name being inscribed with hers on the gravestone.

One would like to think Anne's spirit is freer, in clearer air, than those of her parents and five siblings, immured at mephitic Haworth.

Postscript

Charlotte arranged the installation of the headstone for her sister in St Mary's graveyard, overlooking her beloved Scarborough Sands, with the inscription:

Here
lie the remains of
Anne Brontë
Daughter of the
Revd P. Brontë
Incumbent of Haworth, Yorkshire
She died Aged 28
May 28th 1849

Charlotte's eyes were not sharp enough, however, or were too bleared by tears, to pick up the fact that there were no less than five misprints inscribed on the stone (including Anne's age, which was 29). When Charlotte revisited the grave, three years later, and could (unobserved) get close enough to the stone to read its errors she had it recarved and refaced (the age error she still missed, oddly). The Brontë Society laid a new stone on the grave in 2013.

The original stone, now illegible, was left in place. Anne, its blunders reminds us, was always the neglected one – worth only a cursory glance by posterity.

ATTIC MATTERS

There are obvious objections to the 'Madwoman in the Attic' reading of *Jane Eyre* and the critical theses which have given it currency. Very briefly, the 'Madwoman' theory implies that the 'real' heroine of the novel is the abused, irrepressibly feral woman, Bertha. Call her the 'under-heroine' or, more literally, 'her upstairs'.

The first objection is rather mundane – what one might call the Kirstie Allsopp objection. Bertha Mason is not locked up in an attic. There are indeed attics at Thornfield Hall under the 'leads' (i.e. lead-lined roof). But servants were accommodated in these wretched, cold and leaky dormers at the back of the main building. Bertha Mason is housed in a separate annex, with its own staircase, on the third floor, accessible only by master key, with a barred window.

The second objection is accompanied by the background noise of Charlotte Brontë turning in her grave. The creator of the novel surely did not intend this, superficially perverse, reading – a reading which would take 150 years before anyone tumbled to the 'correct' interpretation of *Jane Eyre*.

Brontë does not pull her punches in describing the first Mrs Rochester – a woman called 'it':

> What it was, whether beast or human being, one could
> not, at first sight, tell: it grovelled, seemingly, on all fours;
> it snatched and growled like some strange wild animal:
> but it was covered with clothing, and a quantity of dark,
> grizzled hair, wild as a mane, hid its head and face.

It was atop the great feminist *erklärung* of the 1960s that Sandra

Gilbert and Susan Gubar, in *The Madwoman in the Attic* (1979), made the point that saw Bertha Mason (few honour her with her married name) become iconic, the quasi-heroine of the novel mis-named *Jane Eyre*.

Using a Freudian 'repression' twist, Gilbert and Gubar argued that Bertha, symbolically, was, if not the 'real' Jane, then her 'other half'. The feral Bertha incarnates the inner rebellion of Victorian womanhood confined within the age's oppressive feminine 'mystique', and the 'maiden' and 'angel in the house' roles, a confinement closer than the corsets which split in half the liver of Charlotte Brontë's disciple, Marie Corelli.

The Madwoman in the Attic argues a powerfully ideological reading and one is grateful for it. But it manifestly violates what Charlotte Brontë, in her ignorance, believed she was doing. What was that? She believed she was writing a 'moral' tale for young women, not a manifesto. When asked what good his novels did, Trollope replied they instructed young women how to receive their suitors. Charlotte Brontë could have said the same. (Emily could not.)

Everyone knows the opening line of *Jane Eyre*: 'There was no possibility of taking a walk that day' and its most famous line: 'Reader, I married him'. Do you, reader, know the last line? 'Amen; even so come, Lord Jesus!'

The Madwoman in the Attic thesis is trotted out, nowadays, in thousands of school and university examination essays. I've read many, with increasing weariness, myself. It is revision critically exhausted by repetition, alongside the similarly worn-out readings of Caliban as the 'real' hero of *The Tempest* and Mr Hyde as the implicitly 'real' hero of Stevenson's novel.

But in a long career I can't recall any essay arguing that *Jane Eyre* is a novel with an overt Christian motive written by a woman who attended church weekly (often daily) and subscribed faithfully to its doctrines; the daughter of a clergyman (whose parsonage she never left – even in death), eventually the wife of a clergyman, who superintended Dorcas meetings,* undertook the routine task of 'district [i.e. parish] visiting' and awaited, with almost orgasmic excitement, the second coming.

That, I venture, might be a truly revisionist reading.

BIGAMY

Like Dorian Gray's picture, the madwoman in the attic is an image which has soared beyond fiction to become iconic. Edward Fairfax Rochester – the Brontëan Bluebeard – keeps the first Mrs Rochester behind bars upstairs. And nobody in the outside world, it would seem, knows she's there – or exists, for that matter. It's not an altogether convenient arrangement for a mentally deranged, enraged, woman with a proclivity for arson and a flame lamp burning day and night in her cell. Appointing a keeper with a weakness for the gin bottle and absent-minded about keys rather risks what convenience there might be.

But the Thornfield Hall arrangement frees the master of the house to enjoy bachelor freedoms and plough his way through 'French countesses, Italian signoras, and German Gräfinnen'.** An offspring from his European dalliances (despite what he protests,

---

* 'Dorcas' being a biblical reference. At these meetings, genteel ladies gathered to sew charity clothes for the poor, while someone (often a minister) read out from holy writings.
** He undertakes this epic philandering across the face of Europe during the Napoleonic Wars.

she must surely be his), Adèle (a French dancer by-blow, presumably), having outgrown the nurse, and before that the wet nurse, requires the attendance of a civilising governess at Thornfield Hall where she (the mad-child of the ground floor) is running riot. It brings Jane Eyre to the Hall. A virtuous young lady, Miss Eyre does not surrender (as many of her subservient kind dutifully would) to her master's sexual interest in her. Marriage is the only way for Edward to have full mastery over Jane.

Before the 1858 Marriage Act bigamy was, social historians tell us, rife. It was divorce, Victorian-style. It's interesting that when Rochester is found, at the altar, in the very act of (attempted) bigamy, no one thinks to summon the local police. 'Just another one' seems to be general view.

Bigamy nonetheless had penalties; but there were virtually insuperable obstacles to divorce. The only legal option, as Dickens's Bounderby explains to Stephen Blackpool (who has his own mad wife) in *Hard Times* (1854), is an Act of Parliament, no less, to cast asunder those whom the Lord hath joined together. Even that was impossible if the spouse were certified mad. Rochester has been careful not to certify Bertha.

The plot of *Jane Eyre* hinges on one of the most melodramatic scenes in Victorian fiction. The marriage ceremony (two deaf and dumb servants recruited, one presumes, as hired witnesses) is interrupted, at the usually perfunctory 'any let or hindrance' point, by a member of the congregation, with a deep sun-tan, who indeed proclaims something of a hindrance. Rochester is married to his living sister, Bertha.

A foiled Rochester conducts the company back to Thornfield Hall, and up the stairs of the private wing to show them his monstrous wife in the flesh. And having been irritatingly denied his bigamous solution, Rochester makes another (un-Christian) suggestion. Jane can, he says, without blessing of clergy, become (common law) wife No. 2. Or, as Jane more bitterly thinks, mistress No. 4, after (Countess) Céline, (Signora) Giacinta, and (Gräfin) Clara. They can live, Rochester blandly suggests, in a plain white cottage in France: he conscientiously respecting her virginal purity, as he would that of a nun. My hunch is that Rochester intends, when the moment is right, to do away with the luckless Bertha, as I believe he eventually does (see below, 'Murder?', page 105).

Jane Eyre and Mr Rochester.
The Brontës, during their lives, did not encourage illustrations. This was done, after their death, by Fred Walker. He is remembered for very fine illustrations to Thackeray and Dickens. The picture reminds how cumbersomely dressed mid-Victorians of the respectable classes were.

This second, quasi-marital, proposal to Jane is in line with Rochester's already established 'Sultanic' character. While lavishing on Jane silk dresses, underwear (we guess) and jewels (which revolt her), in the weeks before their union, he compliments her, chortlingly: 'I would not exchange this one little English girl for the Grand Turk's whole seraglio, gazelle-eyes, houri forms, and all!' The Eastern allusion 'bites' Jane, like an adder. If it is 'houri' (marital whores) he wants, she angrily retorts, let him go to the Stamboul bazaar.

Having given Rochester's polygamous offer some hours' (wavering, chapter-length) thought, Jane runs for the hills – her pearl beyond price preserved for a less improper destiny. There seems to be a Victorian GPS implanted in Miss Eyre's skull, since, exhausted, she collapses on the doorstep of a distant, hitherto unknown, cousin who promptly falls in love with her and, after due religious process, proposes emigration to convert India to Christianity. And Christian monogamy, presumably. St John Rivers should start by converting Thornfield Hall.

BOG PEOPLE

The connection between the Irish and bogs is traditional and traditionally insulting (e.g. 'bog-trotters').* It is calculated some 17 per cent of the country's surface is peat-bog. Patrick, once he went to Cambridge, cut entirely his connection with the 'old sod', his homeland. It was a deliberate act of decontamination. One understands it, but need not admire it. This was the period of the

---

* Bog is one of relatively few words in the English language to have come from Gaelic.

'no Irish need apply' prohibition tacked on to even menial jobs in England. The 1798 uprising was remembered, bitterly. The Irish were primitive and treacherous.

It is likely Patrick was genteelly mocked for his accent at university – something he soon modulated, although a brogue remained, Gaskell observed. It was also distantly detectable, she discerned, in Charlotte's voice.

Patrick seems never to have mentioned, or much communicated with, his sizeable Prunty family – nor the Irish patrons across the sea who got him to Cambridge. None of the children visited the country;* nor, apparently, did they evince the slightest hint of interest in their close family in that country. No Prunty seems ever to have visited Haworth. The Haworth branch seems not to have been concerned by the Great Hunger of the mid-1840s, which must surely have killed, or at least impoverished, some of the Co. Down branch.

Despite this scraping away of the bog stuck to their trotters. Mrs Gaskell refers, high-handedly, to their Irish character. It predisposed, she believed, to hot-headedness. Mrs Humphry Ward, in her haughty introductions to her seven-volume Haworth Edition of all the sisters' published works, positively rants on the Hibernian theme:

> In the first place, has it ever been sufficiently recognised that Charlotte Brontë is first and foremost an *Irishwoman*, that her genius is at bottom a Celtic genius? … The main characteristics indeed of the Celt are all hers – disinterestedness, melancholy, wildness, a wayward force and

---

* Except Charlotte, on her short honeymoon in 1854. She did not, Juliet Barker notes, make any effort to look up her relatives.

passion, for ever wooed by sounds and sights to which
other natures are insensible – by murmurs from the
earth, by colours in the sky, by tones and accents of the
soul, that speak to the Celtic sense as to no other.

In the seven-strong corpus of published Brontë fiction there
is just one memorable Irish character: the gluttonous, brutish
Father Malone, in *Shirley*. No advertisement for the Emerald
Isle, Malone is possessed of none of the high Celtic sensitivities
Mrs Ward eulogises. But he does carry a shillelagh and speak
with an accent the local children mock.

There was an earthier encounter with bog for the Brontës.
A near-death experience with the stuff occurred on 2 September
1824. After a prolonged wet spell there was a day of 'exceeding
fine' weather. Young Emily, Anne, and Branwell prevailed on their
father to let them go for a ramble with the family's two day servants, Nancy and Sarah Garr, local women who knew the area.
Maria, Elizabeth, and Charlotte were at Cowan Bridge (facing,
it would emerge, other lethal dangers).

On the ominously named Crow Hill a sudden storm brewed
up. A violent wind raised gusts of dust and stubble. Lightning
flashed, hailstones rained down. Climactically, close by, Crow Hill
Bog exploded. No overstatement. Boulders were thrown in the
air; mud spewed out in a seven-foot wave and coursed down the
hillside, destroying all in its path.

Led, running, by the Garrs, the children took shelter from
the bog-burst in a porch of Ponden Hall (later immortalised as
Thrushcross Grange). Patrick, back in the parsonage, assumed,
at first, that it was the end of days. Apocalypse. He had always
believed it was imminent. Brave man that he was (he had saved
a drowning boy in his youth) he ran out to rescue his children,

at the risk of his life. He found them, quivering and covered in mud.

Later, Patrick came to believe the bog-burst was caused by earthquake. Geological investigation established it was, in fact, an eruptive subterranean water spout. He persisted in seeing it as the kind of sign predicted in the Book of Revelation. The Lord had rained down bog, as He had once rained down frogs, 'to turn sinners from their ways'. Less theologically, one could see it as a near-miss of death by bog for him and three of his children.

'One wonders,' writes the ever-sober Juliet Barker, 'what effect it had on the children.' One recalls Cathy, in *Wuthering Heights*, running away from Thrushcross Grange (i.e. Ponden Hall), the bulldog Skulker tearing at her heels. (Did the dogs the party took with them to Crow Hill survive, one wonders?)

On the bog theme, Lockwood's description of Gimmerton Churchyard bears close inspection. 'It lies in a hollow, between two hills,' he says, 'an elevated hollow, near a swamp, whose peaty moisture is said to answer all the purposes of embalming on the few corpses deposited there.'

Peaty moisture = bog. The cold, oxygen-free, clammy sub-stance (as in the American 'tar pits') is peculiarly preservative of the dead bodies it contains. This is put forward as the rea-son primitive peoples (including, notably, the Irish) buried certain of their dead in bog. It saved on all those bandages the Egyptians used.

Heathcliff – Linton having just died – bribes the sex-ton to break open Cathy's coffin. Her body has been lying in Gimmerton's 'peaty mould' from March 1784 until August 1801. Heathcliff wrenches off the coffin lid and, as he tells an appalled Nelly, 'I saw her face again – it is hers yet!'. He must be quick to seal the coffin, the sexton warns him. Her face will decompose in front of his eyes 'if the air blew on it'. He arranges that his and Cathy's immutable corpses shall embrace, in the airless peaty mould, forever, never decaying. It's a scene with necrophiliac and vampiric overtones. But it's scientifically sound. Bog preserves. The worm has no kingdom in it.

Gimmerton Sough Kirk is clearly based on Haworth.* The soil there was peaty. Sough means water channel. The graveyard at Haworth, drenched by rain running off the slopes, was, like Gimmerton, swampy.

For the population of Haworth the wetness of their grave-yard created huge problems. It may have preserved their bodies dead; it destroyed them living. It was estimated that by the 1840s 40,000 or more corpses had been deposited in the graveyard, which had no drainage other than run-off via the graves into the springs which fed the water pumps down in the village – most catastrophically, the spring water in the Black Bull pub, which brewed its own beer. One drank corpse in the Bull. Patrick did his best to get the graveyard, into which he deposited some 300 bodies a year, drained, but to no effect.

In recent times, prehistoric bodies, immaculately embalmed, exhumed from Irish bogs, have provided rich hauls for archaeol-ogy – and for the country's greatest poet of recent times. Seamus Heaney's 'bog poems', beginning with 'Bogland' in the 1969 vol-ume *Door Into the Dark*, are written in praise of the substance in which the history of Ireland is most faithfully, most 'livingly', preserved. It is pleasing to note that, thanks to Emily Brontë, Haworth's own bogland has a place in literary history too.

---

* The 'Southowram fallacy', asserting it is based on Chapelle-Beer, near Halifax, is discredited.

Postscript

I cannot help noticing that if you add an umlaut (like that which is found in Brontë) to 'Eyre', rendering it acoustically 'airer', you get 'Eire' – Ireland. Was this a deep code, inserted by Charlotte, to affirm that 'Celtic' identity Mrs Ward rhapsodises about?

BRANDERHAM

When he arrives at Wuthering Heights, flecks of snow falling, wind wuthering, dogs snarling, Lockwood's eye is caught by the 'grotesque carving' over the front of the house. He can make out, 'among a wilderness of crumbling griffins and shameless little boys', the date '1500'. It's an old house and one which quivers, like a cymbal, with past occupants. It has ghosts inside and ghosts outside, Lockwood will learn.

The snow flecks thicken into storm. Lockwood must spend the night in the inhospitable place, where the main entertainment of an evening seems to be hanging puppies. A new servant (Zillah) mistakenly puts the guest in the wrong bedroom: the shrine Heathcliff keeps for the dead (is she?) Cathy to return to when she can find her way into the house. Everyone is already asleep – they rise for the day's work at four.

A bookish fellow, Lockwood reaches out for something to read by the flickering tallow candle he has been left. The Heights is not a bookish house. Foxe's *Book of Martyrs* and *The Pilgrim's Progress* one might expect to be around. Instead of which Lockwood finds an old, leather-bound, privately printed volume. He's curious.

Its inside page is inscribed by the same 'Catherine' who, he had noted, had carved three versions of her surname with a knife on the wooden inside window ledge:

> my eye wandered from manuscript to print. I saw a
> red ornamented title – 'Seventy Time Seven, and the
> First of the Seventy-First. A Pious Discourse delivered
> by the Reverend Jabez Branderham, in the Chapel of
> Gimmerden Sough.' And while I was, half-consciously,
> worrying my brain to guess what Jabes Branderham
> would make of his subject, I sank back in bed, and fell
> asleep.*

Nightmare follows. In it Branderham is rantingly preaching to
'a full and attentive congregation' listening to his interminable
catalogue of the 490 separate sins flesh is heir to. There were,
Lockwood notes, 'odd transgressions that I never imagined previously'. One recalls those 'shameless boys' on the front of the house.

Enraged by Branderham's insistence that, despite mankind's
seven times seventy sinfulness, he Jabes, is one of the elect, and
needs no pardon, Lockwood rises up to denounce him for his
antinomian heresy.** Jabes summarily instructs the congregation
to kick the stranger to death, which they set about doing.

It's a very odd way to begin a novel. One can make sense of
it by thinking about where 'Ellis Bell' wrote it. The Haworth

---

* The number seven, and its multiples, is everywhere in the Book of
Revelation – not, one suspects, Lockwood's favourite bedtime reading
matter.
** Emily would have been long familiar with antinomianism (invinci-
ble salvation, whatever one's sinfulness) from the children's delight in
their favourite novel, James Hogg's *Memoirs and Confessions of a Justified
Sinner*.

chapel dated back at least to the 14th century. Over the next half millennium it went through various restorations. But it was never very much of a place – just a 'chapelry of ease' in the vast parish of Bradford (everything is big in Yorkshire).

It was inconvenient to carry corpses the four miles or more to the city's burial grounds. And corpses were what Haworth produced as efficiently as Preston manufactured cotton. The church graveyard (see above, 'Bog people', page 11) was estimated to contain 44,000 bodies – bodies which, perversely, did not rot as they would elsewhere, in decent, God-fearing dirt. Dead Haworthians were routinely buried ten feet down in the soggy, boggy earth, to make room for neighbours above.

Haworth was the necropolis of the north-west. The one visit the Archbishop of York, the chapel's nominal head, is recorded as making, during Patrick's decades of curacy, was to consecrate ground for the enlargement of the graveyard. More corpse-room.

Haworth church

The parsonage, with the graveyard in the foreground.

Age expectancy, for the 60 per cent who were lucky (or unlucky) enough to survive infancy, was in the low twenties.

Nor was the curacy beneficent. Patrick was hired on a £60 p.a. stipend. This pittance was exacted from the local population, through their tight-fisted church committee who did not all think that their new curate was worth more than £5 a month. On arrival, before death thinned their numbers, the Brontës were a family of eight, with full-time servants in attendance. Sixty pounds a year would barely keep eight sheep alive.

But the parsonage, the building they would live, write, and die in, was exceedingly fine. It was a spacious Georgian mansion constructed in the 1770s: the era of Britain's finest Neoclassical architecture. It is currently, with some small enlargement, the Brontë Parsonage Museum.

The Brontës were paupers and charity children (no decent education could be afforded them) who found themselves living in a house a mill-owner in Bradford might envy. It created that condition of strange social anomaly which runs through their lives and fiction. Why were such brilliant women 'governesses' (upper servants)? Why was such a brilliant young man as Branwell a railway clerk? Why did they not 'rise'?

How to explain this anomaly? And how to explain the grand house? The Revd William Grimshaw (undoubtedly the inspiration for Jabes Branderham) is the answer. Grimshaw (1708–1763) was the clergyman who made pre-Brontë Haworth famous. And he achieved that fame for himself and his town by fire-and-brimstone preaching. When he came to the Haworth chapel, in the early 1740s, he reported to the Archbishop that the attendance on a Sunday was a dozen communicants. Pitiful. One of the great Anglican revivalists of the century at the peak of his career, Grimshaw would enthral, in open air-services, as many as 1,000 congregants and 500 communicants. He did brisk 'cottage services' by the dozen a day. He was a sermonising whirlwind.

A Sabbatarian of savage enthusiasm (he ended, forever, Haworth's Sunday football, drunken 'wakes', horseracing and other hellish dissipation), Grimshaw would, legend had it, drive any recalcitrant worshippers into the church with a horsewhip. Since, thanks to him, there was no other entertainment of a Sunday than his sermons he probably did not need the whip. He was, portraits confirm, a large, burly, man.

He also had a brain. What Grimshaw shrewdly realised was that Methodism was spreading like wildfire through the decayed parochial institutions of the Anglican Church by virtue of one dynamic thing. Sermons. The faithful did not want sub-Latinate liturgy or psalms – they liked it hot. Grimshaw was a master of the 'market' dialect which got across to his listeners. He preached up to 30 times a week, using the Methodists' own winning formula.

Grimshaw's style was histrionic. He was, says his curt entry in the *Oxford Dictionary of National Biography*, an 'alarming' preacher. Most alarming was his sermon on 2 September 1744 when, mid-service (the second of the day) he collapsed, foaming, in the pulpit. He was thought dead, but, like Lazarus, William Grimshaw came back to report he had been in the third heaven. The reference was to 2 Corinthians where Paul recalls:

> I know a man in Christ who fourteen years ago was caught up to the third heaven ... He heard inexpressible things, things that man is not permitted to tell.

It was not all ecstasy, histrionics and day trips to paradise. A shrewd ecclesiastical tactician, Grimshaw formed working alliances with local Methodists. The strength of the Anglican Church was ceremonial: it could christen, marry, and bury. But it could not, as successfully as its rival, inflame. An ecumenical modus vivendi was possible.

Grimshaw lived in a run-down 'cottage' of grotesque shabbiness in the aptly named Sowdens Crossroads (the name could be taken to mean 'sty of pigs'), deep in Haworth valley. Its water pump discharged Haworth's usual attar of corpse and human filth – and bacilli. Grimshaw, otherwise hale, died a young 54 of typhus. All his family – wife and children – died before him of the same water-borne disease. Care of souls was one thing, but care of sewers might have served Haworth better.

It was Grimshaw's achievement, and what he had done for the Church in the Haworth area, which encouraged the archbishopric to invest in the anomalously fine parsonage. It was, alas, opened ten years too late for Grimshaw himself. High up the valley slope, the new parsonage enjoyed pure moorland water.

It meant that the Brontës could die of the 'poets' disease', TB, not putrid typhus which killed their predecessor and his family.

William Grimshaw has no monument in Haworth. Emily's 'Jabes Branderham' will have to serve. Oh, and for those who think about it, the parsonage.

BRANWELL'S ROBINSONIAD

'My brilliant boy', Patrick called his one and only son. Brilliant but doomed. Before being terminally incapacitated by drink, drugs, self-pity and sexual incontinence, Branwell had written – as he told his closest friend in September 1845 – the first volume of a three-decker novel. There were four Brontës at the parsonage pulling away at the same oar around this period. A veritable fiction factory.

The plot of what Branwell was writing was clear in his mind. It would be what the Victorians called 'a novel with a purpose'. The three volumes would be Branwell's testament: chronicling a fall like Lucifer's, precipitated, like Adam's *felix culpa*, by a woman and a serpent. The name of the villainess? Mrs Robinson. It would be something sensational.

Whatever Branwell put on paper was, one presumes, destroyed in the ruthless purge of literary remains Charlotte carried out after the last of her siblings died, leaving her to fashion the Brontës' literary legacy as she saw fit and prudent. Branwell's *Robinsoniad* (let's call it that) probably went to the bonfire, along with bundles of indiscreet letters, journals, a quantity of Emily's poetry and, quite feasibly, her mythic follow-up to *Wuthering Heights*. Charlotte's motives for this destruction have never

A fine silhouette of Branwell. Such pictures were made mechanically.

been explained but they can be surmised (see below, 'Survivor's Privileges', page 152).

His story contained, Branwell confided to his drinking pal, the unvarnished account of his disastrous love affair with the sirenic 'Mrs R.', as Charlotte called her, unable to speak the Jezebel's name. Patrick called her the 'diabolical seducer'.

Branwell, as anyone who knew him confirmed, was formidably talented but he was woefully uneducated in any formal sense. Money being short, he had been home-tutored by Patrick, in the father's few hours of spare time, with the hope that like his father, Branwell could overcome formidable obstacles and make it to university. In the event he couldn't.

Branwell was clever, had gifts as an artist and poet, but he fell somewhat short, on the evidence that survives, of 'brilliance'. Emily was the better artist; Charlotte was infinitely better with words and more organised intellectually. Both were more diligent autodidacts. So, too, in her reticent way, was Anne.

He collaborated with his sisters on the Angria/Gondal sagas – those fascinating juvenile and adolescent 'wonderlands' the Brontë children created in their Haworth years (Emily was still dabbling in them as an adult). Angria – a region in the Verdopolitan (Glass town) Federation – was largely the creation of Charlotte and Branwell; the stories reveal a precocious interest in colonialism. Emily and Anne's Gondal, on the other hand, is less interested in wonderland than male heroism: supermen of the time such as Napoleon and Wellington, whose mythology feeds into Heathcliff, Rochester, et al.

In later life Branwell complained that the 'petting' he had received, as the hope of the Brontës, rendered him constitutionally idle. It was one of his more honest self-assessments. The infant Emily (around seven years old) was asked by her father what she would do for Branwell, 'who was sometimes a naughty boy'. She answered 'reason with him, and when he won't listen to reason whip him'. It worked with her dog. Who knows, it might have worked with her brother.

Like all the writing Brontës, Branwell revered the author of *Don Juan* and was a would-be Byronist. But he lacked (to his credit, some might say) the Byronic ruthlessness in his dealings with women. As an art student in Leeds, and practising artist in Bradford, he hung out with a loose crowd who probably talked more fornication than they got. Scarce Haworth funds were squandered on booze and doxies. He probably developed laddish ideas about sex which would last all his short life.

It would be interesting to know what Branwell was like in drink. Accounts suggest he was a roisterer: a life-and-soul kind of man. One thing is demonstrable: he bought more rounds than he could pay for. Debts to public houses (notably the Old Cock – interesting name) brought, in the months of his downfall, bailiffs all the way from Bradford to the parsonage door. Most biographers credit a friend's comment that Branwell fathered at least one bastard child on a luckless servant girl. It may have been the cause of his dismissal from his first (quickly terminated) job as a private tutor.

Dismissal was to be a recurrent entry on the Branwell CV. He failed as a portrait painter to Bradford's self-regarding *nouveaux riches* and failed as a clerk in the booming railway business which was laying down a modern transport network in the industrial north. Patrick fondly hoped his son would become a captain of industry, if he couldn't be the next Gainsborough. But the Leeds and Manchester Company job lasted less than a year. There was the faint suspicion of peculation in his departure. Or it may have been incompetence – the arithmetic Patrick taught him was perhaps as patchy as his spelling. Whatever the offence, summary dismissal followed. The magazines (*Blackwood's*, notably) and eminent writers (Wordsworth and Southey, notably) he bombarded with his verse and ill-written demands for employment were politely dismissive. Sometimes less than politely.

By 1842 Patrick Branwell Brontë was at a very loose end. Emily cared for him sparingly (doubtless she still thought whipping would help). Charlotte considered him a cross she had to bear. He had manifestly failed the father whose names he bore. Shame was making him reckless.

Anne, the most caring of the sisters where Branwell was concerned, finally found something for him. Herself now a governess with the Robinson family at Thorp Green Hall, near York, she had charge of the two younger daughters. The family, headed by the Revd Edmund Robinson, was wealthy. The country house was rather more grand than Haworth Parsonage (as noted elsewhere, it is immortalised as Horton Lodge, in *Agnes Grey*).

The comfortable lodging was more congenial to Anne than was Thorp Green's free and easy moral atmosphere within it. The head of the house was, if we credit Anne's novel, a hunting and drinking parson. His younger wife, Lydia, was, if we credit the novel, 'dashing'. Coming from a Brontë it was not a term of praise.

There had been an elopement scandal with one of the older girls. The younger two daughters, Anne's teenaged charges, were, the novel hints, flighty. Keeping them in line was a battle for Anne. The son and heir, Edmund Jr, had been last to arrive. With him in the world Mrs Robinson's marital duty was done. Now, aged eight, the young man needed a tutor to prepare him for school and university. On Anne's recommendation Branwell was recruited. It was a comfortable berth. He had his own apartment and his tutorial duties were light and, having been home-tutored himself, easily handled.

There is a veil of obscurity over how, as he always did, Branwell went off the rails. It may have been drink. He may have taken liberties (welcomed perhaps) with the younger Robinson women. A paedophiliac interest in young Edmund has been unconvincingly hypothesised. Possibly some financial misdemeanour was committed (he was a good enough artist to forge signatures). One would like to think not.

What is known from surviving records is that the precipitating cause of the disaster was (alleged) misconduct with (complicit?) Mrs Robinson. Forty-three when Branwell arrived, Lydia Robinson was, supposedly, sexually appetitive, and 'damnably' fond of him, Branwell wrote to a friend. She was also cultivated and connected to the highest echelons of Whig politics through her brother, Thomas Gisborne, MP for Nottingham. Thorp Green, and a maternal role, may have been stiflingly boring for her.

The handsome, clever, malleable young tutor could satisfy Lydia's middle-aged restlessness. But Branwell never registered the fact that the worldly Lydia had no intention of ever throwing herself away on the penniless son of a penniless curate. He himself had used some servant girl: an upper servant that he was, he too would receive the same kind of using. If he were lucky, more gently and profitably.

A scenario can be reconstructed from Branwell's later, frantic letters. There are those who think his account of the Thorp Green imbroglio so much fantasy. There are others, a majority, who think them essentially true: he was taken advantage of. Seventeen years older than he, Lydia Robinson was possessed, Branwell believed, of 'totally unselfish generosity, sweet temper and unwearied care for all others'. She was brutally treated, she gave him to understand, 'by an eunuch like fellow who though possessed of such a treasure never even occupied the same apartment with her'. The Revd Robinson, that was to say.

No eunuch he, Branwell, it would seem, furtively shared the apartment (or she his) and 'had daily "troubled pleasure soon chastised by fear"* in the society of one whom I must, till death, call my wife.' This for three years, he told his confidant,

---

* The quotation is from Pope's translation of the *Iliad*, Book VI. Branwell was doubtless teaching it to Edmund. The surrounding passage describes Hector's tender departure from his wife, Andromache. Branwell as Hector is a bit of a pull.

and boozing friend, Francis Grundy. The blunt rejoicing in his superior sexual potency suggests that, by some strangely inverted theology Branwell conceived adultery, as he experienced it, as a kind of marriage: solemnised by his loins.

What strains credulity is that for three years the affair was not noticed – at least by the cuckolded head of the household to whom the servants reported. Where was the affair going, if there was an affair? Divorce was only possible by an Act of Parliament. Unlikely. Elopement would mean life without servants. Even more unlikely. Lydia would have to be very much in love (and much younger) to give up the amenities of Thorp Green Hall.

In an ideal world, death would soon enough carry off Lydia's 'bloodless mock husband', as Branwell called him, clearing the way for his successor. No question who that should be (in Branwell's mind). The Revd Robinson was, as it happened, ill and the medical forecast was dire. Branwell, fool that he was, saw himself as the future master of Thorp Green. He wrote confidently to his friend, Grundy, about 'The probability of [Robinson's] state of health ere long leaving [Lydia] free to give me herself and her estate.' It is hard to forgive Branwell for that calculation about usurping another man's 'estate' (not to mention his wife).

The nearness of York Minster, and the annual holidays in blissful Scarborough had been the happiest things in Anne's short, emotionally restricted life. But the Thorp Green delinquency sorely chafed her moral sensibility. She must surely have tried to bring her brother to his senses. Where Mrs Robinson was concerned he was evidently senseless.

Anne remained five years, until Branwell's misdoings made further staying impossible, and she resigned her post, in June

1845, before the crisis came. 'During my stay [at Thorp Green]', she confided to her diary, 'I have had some very unpleasant and undreamt of experience of human nature'. In the margin of her prayer book she jotted that human beings now disgusted her. Animals ('the lesser creation') she could still love.

Her two girls, flibbertigibbets that they were (one suspects), now in their nubile late teens, loved Anne, even after the Branwell disaster. And they gave her what would be one of her dearest possessions: the puppy 'Flossy' (see below, page 50). Everyone who came close to her loved Anne, it seems. She could have stayed, not as a governess to her now adult charges but as a salaried companion, until they got married. Things might have worked out well for her – perhaps, as in *Agnes Grey*, some suitor as eligible (and preferably high church) as the Revd Weston might have come her way, having perceived Miss Brontë's quiet worth.

The havoc Branwell precipitated, as the Robinson imbroglio came to a head, is outlined in the few desperate letters of his which survive, in guardedly oblique remarks in his sisters' correspondence, and in Mrs Gaskell's tendentious (and, as it turned out, libellous) account. Whatever hopes Lydia raised in foolish Branwell, she was not foolish enough to disinherit herself. Her husband was not so sick that he could not, as his last act on his deathbed if need be, change his will. And her children were not so loving to Anne that they would welcome Branwell Brontë as their step-papa.

Someone (a Thorp Green gardener, one version has it) told Edmund what had been going on for years under his nose, shortly after Anne left. A savage letter was dispatched to Branwell, taking a summer break at Haworth, threatening to shoot him out of hand should he venture to Thorp Green. The hunting parson had that much life left in him. The Revd Robinson did not, however, change his will, which left Lydia the bulk of the family's sizeable wealth and property.

One can only speculate what self-serving version of events Lydia invented to mollify her husband. Most likely it was one which cast Branwell as a fantasist. He had misunderstood Mrs Robinson's, his employer's, courtesies as covert passion. He was a madman. He had made it all up, to extort money from the family.

Branwell waited impatiently at Haworth, stupefying himself with drink, opium and wild dreams of things working out his way. Lydia clandestinely sent him sums of money. They kept his hopes alive, and the Black Bull public house, down the hill from the parsonage (it's still there), busy.

The Revd Robinson duly died, ten months later, in May 1846. Fury against Branwell may have accelerated his demise. The way should now, Branwell thought, have been open for him to return

The Black Bull

and claim his love and her wealth. The way was not open. In fact it was permanently barred. He was told, by responsible third parties, that Lydia herself was dangerously ill, 'insane' with grief and emotional confusion. Branwell's letters were, apparently, returned unopened.

Branwell was subsequently given to understand, by increasingly cold (dis)missives, that Robinson's will excluded his wife from any posthumous benefit in the event of her not breaking off, entirely, any relationship present or future with Patrick Branwell Brontë. She was obliged to do that.

The business about the clause in the will was not true; and if true it would never have been enforceable. Like Edward Casaubon's posthumous prohibition against Ladislaw's marrying the widowed Dorothea in *Middlemarch*, English law would laugh at such 'dead hand' control over the living.

Branwell evidently believed his true love was being persecuted and held in vile bondage by the terms of her dead spouse's cruel will. He further stupefied himself on what she sent and whatever he could scrounge, or steal, from the parsonage (or get on credit from the Black Bull and the local apothecary, both of whom knew the money would come from the family, if not him). There's an unpleasant reference in one of Charlotte's letters to his cheating his father out of a sovereign.

Branwell was paralysed, totally inert, as Charlotte told Ellen Nussey, bitterly:

> Branwell declares now that he neither can nor will do anything for himself – good situations have been offered more than once – for which by a fortnight's work he might have qualified himself – but he will do nothing – except drink and make us all wretched.

Why did Lydia send him money to drink himself paralytic? It's absurd to think that Branwell was blackmailing the woman he so foolishly, and genuinely, loved. And if he tried to threaten her with exposure Thorp Green men with horsewhips would have joined the bailiffs at the parsonage door. Nor is it easy to credit that, 'diabolical' as she may have been, Lydia hoped to precipitate his death by encouraging toxic overdose – although that was what was happening. He was drinking and drugging himself to death.

The most likely explanation is that she feared the stupid young fellow would kill himself. It was the same reason, in his last weeks, his father slept overnight in the same bed with Branwell. They must have been troubled nights.

The folderol about the prohibitive clause in the will was a smokescreen, Lydia's enemies assert. The cunning widow had a plan in which Branwell had no place. Edmund Robinson died at the end of May 1846. Eighteen months later, Lydia had resourcefully won the heart of Sir Edward Dolman Scott: some 27 years older than she, now a rather less 'dashing' 48. Sir Edward had a conveniently dying spouse (what love potion did the woman have? Or, horrible gothic thought, killing potion).

Lady Scott (daughter of the evangelically named Temperance Gisborne) was Lydia's cousin. Lydia the widow was there to console the widower. She must have done it deftly. She became, by private licence, the second Lady Scott at the end of 1848.

By this time the rejected Branwell had lost all will to live and had died, a sot and an addict, at the end of September 1848. Whether he was buried still wearing on his chest the lock of hair Lydia had given him in happier days is not recorded. It would all have made a good novel. But he never completed that, any more than he succeeded at anything in his life.

BRANWELL'S ROBINSONIAD II

Lydia's story

She was, Mrs Gaskell bluntly declared, 'a bad woman'. According to Charlotte, 'a worse woman, I might say I believe, hardly exists – the more I hear of her the more deeply she revolts me'.

How bad and revolting was she? Some rearguard defence – as with Benjamin Braddock's Mrs Robinson in *The Graduate* – can be mounted. Lydia Gisborne (what Branwell always called her, annulling her marriage verbally) came from a wealthy, politically active, ecclesiastically powerful family which had been distinguished gentry and clerisy for generations in Derbyshire.

In addition to large land-holdings the Gisbornes had industrial interests in coal, lime and sand in Manchester – building materials and fuel required in ever-increasing quantities during the industrial revolution. Lydia's clergyman father was one of the moving spirits behind the evangelical revolution, the so-called 'Clapham Sect', which transformed the 19th-century Anglican Church. He was notable.

William Wilberforce, even more notable, was a frequent guest at Thomas Gisborne Snr's home. There were family connections with Thomas Babington Macaulay. It is hard to believe some of the high domestic culture did not rub off on Lydia (named after her mother and the younger of the two daughters in the family). Her background in the elite Victorian intelligentsia must have had magnetic appeal to Branwell.

Lydia's elder brother, Thomas Gisborne the Younger (1789–1852), went on to become a noted, if rather scatty MP of the Reform Party. Lydia must have brought money to her marriage with Robinson – which, by the law of the land, became her husband's. But she also brought, by virtue of her name, distinction; and, one guesses, intellectual liveliness.

Branwell's allegations of marital incompatibility may have been well founded. What he meant by the husband's 'brutality' is unknowable. Lydia may not have wanted five children, but a son (the fifth to arrive) was required of her. Thereafter her bedroom (as Branwell observed), and her body, were her own.

One can easily imagine that Thorp Green was, for Lydia, a stultifying environment compared to that she grew up in. She was, one suspects, pre-menopausal. Branwell was flattering diversion and reassurance she still had sexual charm. He was widely read and 'Byronic' (he hoped). And, as he implicitly boasts, he may have been a lusty lover.

Once widowed, Lydia could escape to a larger world than Thorp Green. That world was not the Haworth Parsonage. Sir Edward Dolman Scott, a baronet, owned extensive land in Great Barr. He was also enriched by lime-works. This was one of the industrial lines in which the Gisbornes also had a commercial interest. There were probably longstanding family, social and business connections, which would explain the speed of the second marriage between Lydia and Sir Edward, and the ease with which the mutually widowed couple slipped into it.

A grandee and a magnate, Sir Edward had had a long, if silent, career in Parliament as a Whig with occasional radical tendencies. Although Charlotte Brontë called him Lydia's 'infatuated slave', the disposition of his property after death was anything but reckless. He died, at his family seat in Great Barr, in December 1851. His will had been made a few months earlier. It suggested the marriage was more pragmatic than blissful.

Lydia was left a meagre £600 a year life annuity. The family estates went entirely, with the baronet's title, to the eldest son. If she were an adventuress (she probably wasn't) Lydia had gambled for high stakes and lost. But she still had the wealth her first husband had left her. She lived on, twice widowed, for decades, never publicly disclosing the truth of the Branwell affair, despite provocations. It was not until after her death that Mrs Gaskell's unvarnished account of what had happened at Thorp Green Hall was published.

Mrs Gaskell had told her publisher, the ever-loyal George Smith, before publication that she positively relished a libel suit from the 'bad woman' of Thorp Green Hall. Lady Scott's lawyers promptly obliged when the biography was published, in 1857.

Gaskell's account was, as she had warned Smith, ostentatiously libellous. It was a gamble and ultimately Smith lost his nerve. All unsold copies of the first edition had to be recalled. The second edition was purged of reference, by lawyer's direction. A humiliating 'letter of retraction' was published in *The Times*. No legally worthwhile substantiation of Branwell's conduct could be found to mitigate the shame. Luckily no younger member of the Brontë family was alive to feel the shame. Patrick must have.

The humiliating revisions to the biography, and the 'retraction', branded Branwell not the victim of a designing woman, as he was in the suppressed first edition, but a downright fantasist, aided by an irresponsible biographer. A minority verdict would believe, to this day, that was exactly what he was. One longs for the unwritten novel – or, at least, the first volume Charlotte destroyed.

BUMPS ON THE HEAD

Mrs Gaskell gives a vivid snapshot ('a good look') of her first meeting with the then-34-year-old Charlotte Brontë. It has a livingness quite unlike the few lifetime portraits done by Branwell and others which have survived.

> I went up to unbonnet, etc.; came down to tea; the little lady worked away and hardly spoke but I had time for a good look at her. She is (as she calls herself) *undeveloped*, thin, and more than half a head shorter than I am; soft brown hair, not very dark; eyes (very good and expressive, looking straight and open at you) of the same colour as her hair; a large mouth; the forehead square, broad and rather over-hanging.

The forehead – which sounds a trifle Cro-Magnon – is, for thoughtful Victorians, a most telling detail.

On 29 June 1851, on one of her rare excursions to London, Charlotte went with her publisher, George Smith (under the alias Mr and Miss Fraser), to the phrenologist Dr J.P. Browne, whose surgery was in Cadogan Square. Trained in Edinburgh, Browne was, doubtless, a disciple of the most famous Scoto-British phrenologist, George Combe (1788–1858).

Smith kept Browne's long and detailed 'Phrenological Estimate of the Talents and Dispositions of a Lady'. To draw it up, the phrenologist would have 'felt' with his fingers the head beneath her soft brown hair – erotically, almost, as his knowing fingers passed and pressed over the salient, anterior and superior areas of 'Miss Fraser's' skull. He would also have calipered the dimensions and sketched it.

Her cranial configuration, Browne determined, was:

> very remarkable. The forehead is at once very large and well formed. It bears the stamp of deep thoughtfulness

and comprehensive understanding. It is highly philo-
sophical. It exhibits the presence of an intellect at once
perspicacious and perspicuous.

A perceptive verdict, it might seem. For good measure, he added,
'If not a poet her sentiments are poetical'.

However, what Browne reported on 'Miss Fraser' was,
accounts of him in the *Phrenological Journal* suggest, a usual line
in flattering patter and the discovery of 'remarkable' features.
He was, like most of his kind, more interested in guineas than
science.

Psychologists dismiss phrenology as quackery – along with
Victorian table-rapping, 'animal magnetism', and astrological
readings of character (all of which the Brontës subscribed to).
But, at the level of folklore, we retain a loyalty to Dr Browne's
discredited 'science' in terms such as 'highbrow'.

The Victorians were peculiarly interested in cranial size
and often weighed brains postmortem. Brontë's idol, Thackeray,
weighed in at a massive 58.5oz. The grey matter dwarfed that
of Walt Whitman – a mere 44oz – but was, alas for England,
dwarfed by Turgenev's jumbo 70oz.

However dubiously he got there, Dr Browne's cerebral
anatomisation hit the nail on the head, so to speak. The report
confirmed Charlotte's faith in the pseudo-science, which she introduced prominently ('headfirst', one might say) into her fiction.

At her interview with Mme Beck (in *Villette*), Lucy, for
example, is 'read' physiognomically (digital investigation of her
skull being, probably, a step too far). This was easier with men of
years. The Victorian cult of male baldness (while approving the
beard) was a way of giving prominence to the brow, as something
proudly displayed.

Characters in Brontë's fiction are often defined as rattling bags of cranial 'organs'. In Chapter 4 of *Shirley* we are told:

> Mr. Yorke, in the first place, was without the organ of Veneration – a great want, and which throws a man wrong on every point where veneration is required. Secondly, he was without the organ of Comparison – a deficiency which strips a man of sympathy; and, thirdly, he had too little of the organs of Benevolence and Ideality, which took the glory and softness from his nature, and for him diminished those divine qualities throughout the universe.

As for the 'little woman' (to borrow Mrs Gaskell's term)? The forehead must tell all.

THE CONFESSION BOX

It is instructive to dig a little deeper into the plot of *Villette*, in those places where one can test what the fiction portrays against the (frustratingly fragmentary) factual record of Charlotte's sojourn in Brussels. (I've wrestled, vainly, with why she pseudonymised that fine capital city as 'little town'. Probably every Belgian schoolchild knows.)

A prime example of where fact can be tested against the novel's fiction is the extraordinary scene in which Lucy, in the throes of her illicit passion for Paul Emanuel – as the author herself had been to her *maître* in Brussels, Constantin Héger – submits herself to Catholic confession.

There is high tension around the scene: will Lucy, in the

extremity of her uncontrollable desires (and, possibly, opium), fall prey to the Whore of Rome? Charlotte, inflamed by her feelings for Constantin, herself took Catholic confession, on 1 September 1843, in the Brussels Church (now a cathedral) of St Michael and St Gudula. Belgian Brontëans (an indefatigably resourceful crew) have identified the very confessional box (a wildly florid structure) in which Charlotte, defying every tenet of Haworth, found her most unusual audience.

Charlotte confided to Emily what happened in a surprisingly skittish (given the seriousness of her act) letter. The priest, on learning the English lady on the other side of the *grille* was Protestant, quite properly declined to receive her confession. Eventually, after her beseeching him to do so, he relented, in the hope, as he said, that it would bring her back to the 'true church' (truth in short supply in Haworth's Chapel of Ease, evidently; the Revd Patrick Brontë would have snorted indignantly).

In the novel the confessor is the wily Père Silas. His characterisation borrows strongly from 1840s and 1850s anti-Jesuit paranoia, depicted, melodramatically, in innumerable novels of 'faith and doubt' of that period. It was not all low-grade propagandistic fiction. Brontë's other *maître*, Thackeray, introduced a subtle Jesuit into *Henry Esmond*, a couple of years before *Villette*.

Fear of Jesuits, and the Catholic Church generally, had been raised to paranoid levels by Newmanism and the Oxford movement* in the 1840s and by the 'Papal Aggression' of 1851, when

---

* John Henry Newman, later Cardinal Newman, was the most famous of the Anglicans who 'went across' to Rome. He resigned his position at Oxford University to do so and took a number of his collegians with him.

Rome decided to 'establish' itself in Britain, with a national hierarchy. John Bull raged.

What on earth induced Charlotte Brontë to expose her soul to a Catholic priest at this fraught period? James Tully claims (in his uncompromisingly titled docufiction *Crimes of Charlotte Brontë*) that 'the indications' are that Charlotte and M. Héger 'eventually became lovers in every sense of the word'. Tully assumes Charlotte was so weighed down with guilt at her adultery, 'she had to unburden herself' – if not to her church, then to Héger's. It would ease her conscience if she could divulge her sin to someone who, by the disciplines of his church, could never pass on her confession.

One doesn't give this scenario too much credence. But there are, undeniably, hints of pervasive sexual guilt in the eerie history of the *pensionnat Beck* in *Villette* (based, closely, on the Héger institution in Rue d'Isabelle). Its dormitories were once nuns' cells (ambiguous word). In the garden there is a tree where, whispered legend among the girls had it, a nun who had defiled her vows of chastity had been buried alive. Her ghost walked. Or so the pupils tell each other.

The Héger girls (those Belgian Brontëans, again, have established) often had, as their breakfast, fruit – pears, when in season – plucked from the garden, marinaded in wine. The pear tree was very old; it must have been there in the days of the convent, and the luckless nun. What did the tree roots clutch and suck in the depths of the soil?

My own feeling is that Charlotte was drawn to the Catholic Church, as many have been, by the beauty of its décor, its venerable ritual, its Latin, its authority – headed as it is by the most powerful father figure in the world. There are hints elsewhere in the fiction of a pull to Rome: in *Shirley*, for example, with its remarks on the opening page about Protestant baptism resembling a hasty ablution in a bedroom ewer.

Like Anne (who felt a similar attraction to the magnificence of York Minster) Charlotte's sensibility was, one can surmise, occasionally unfulfilled by the pragmatic simplicity of Haworth: a 'holy' place where local women hung their washing out to dry on the gravestones (Patrick tolerated them doing it: he wrote an amused poem about vests on the stones).

The immensely well-informed editor of Charlotte's letters, Margaret Smith, pooh-poohs fanciful speculation about any sexual peccadilloes with Héger or temptations to 'go over' in the confession box. Charlotte's act was, Smith asserts, a high-spirited 'experiment'. Nothing more. As she described it in her letter to Emily 'it was only a freak'. Adding, however, 'don't tell father'. Wise warning.

CREOLE

Bertha Mason-Rochester's irruption into the narrative is the most dramatic moment in *Jane Eyre*'s action. It's somewhat spoilt by the fact that modern readers will probably know what's coming. One envies those first readers of October 1847 for whom the madwoman in the attic was an unexpected bombshell.

Latter-day readers, however, have taken new, and more speculative lines of interpretation. Bertha's entry on the scene tends nowadays to be seen as more complex than a *coup de théâtre* and what G.H. Lewes (Charlotte Brontë's favourite critic) called *mélodrame*. It points to things much larger than the world of Thornfield.

Bertha's marital/sexual degradation at the hands of Rochester, modern critical thinking proposes, is of global significance. She is, Sandra Gilbert and Susan Gerber, argue:

> The Jamaican Creole whose racial and geographical marginality oils the mechanism by which the heathen, bestial Other could be annihilated to constitute European female subjectivity.

One wonders whether Charlotte would have liked that critical phraseology as much as she liked the Gallic suavities of G.H. Lewes. But in a modern, post-colonial, post-racial world it's a thought-provoking observation by Gilbert and Gubar.

There is, however, a problem. If, like the (odious) Apartheid-era policeman one tries to work out what precise fraction of Bertha is 'black' or 'mixed race' and what fraction 'European', things get blurry.

'Creole', the epithet applied to Bertha, generally denotes 'patois-speaking', not racial origin. Jamaicans have a particularly rich creole dialect which is now recognised in some quarters as an actual language. It has, via immigration (and the popularity of reggae artists like Bob Marley), enriched contemporary British vernacular speech.

Historically 'creoles' were largely white colonials who had adapted in their speech, chameleon-like, to their surroundings – not colonials sexually intermixed with native inhabitants. Nonetheless, the term *could* mean that. It's vague.

Bertha is never given a word of speech in the novel (she had to wait for Jean Rhys, in *Wide Sargasso Sea* to verbalise her). It would be interesting to know how she talks. She is described by Jane as 'tall, dark, and majestic'. No specific ascription of mixed race is made. Her pigmentation is 'dark'; her brother Richard's is 'sallow'. That could, as Jane thinks, mean exposure to sun – or, we might think, some strain of Afro-Jamaican ancestry.

There is one shred of hard evidence. Rochester tells Jane that Bertha's family wanted him to marry her not simply to dispose of a bad seed (nymphomaniac daughter of a mad mother) but because 'I was of good race'. So was she, on her side, of 'bad' race? Rochester later adds:

> Bertha Mason is mad [because] she came of a mad family; – idiots and maniacs through three generations! Her mother, the Creole, was both a mad woman and a drunkard!

It hints at intermarriage, in the now-distant past. But blood will out. Bertha, we are told is labelled 'creole' on her marriage certificate, which seems odd. The implication, never quite confirmed, is that Bertha was the daughter of a woman who was noteworthily different – culturally or racially – from her husband, the patriarchal and rich plantation owner, Mr Mason.

Charlotte Brontë (cunningly, I would like to think) leaves it all up in the air. As does Emily with Heathcliff's origins. Is he black, Gipsy, Irish? All three hypotheses have been tried out: none rings quite true. He, too, would leave our Apartheid-era inspector scratching his head.

DATES

Call up a selection of the greatest Victorian novels written by Victorian women and *Middlemarch* probably heads the list, followed, one might confidently hazard, by *Jane Eyre* and *Wuthering Heights*.

Are they, however, *Victorian* novels? Yes and no. Yes they are Victorian in that they were all published during the reign of the most powerful woman in the world – Queen and Empress. No, they are not Victorian, in that they all practise that unique literary habit of the period, narrative antedating. *Middlemarch*, for example, published in the early 1870s, is set, historically, in the period before and shortly after the 1832 Reform Act.

Many have tried but no critic has persuasively explained the Victorian novelists' widespread practice of retro-narration. It may be homage to that archetypal 19th-century work, Scott's *Waverley*, with its subtitle, *'Tis Sixty Years Since*. Some have suggested that the Victorian era was changing so fast that novelists went back, often to the period of their birth and childhood, in nostalgic reminiscence of historical stability: the way things were. Living in the present, said the Victorian novelist Charles Reade, was like travelling on a runaway express train.

Trollope (unlike his idol, Thackeray, an inveterate ante-dater) is the exception. When Trollope wrote *The Way We Live Now*, he meant it. He published the work in the early 1870s, and that is precisely (and dateably) when the action of the novel is set. For most others it was the way we lived then.

When, then, is *Jane Eyre* set? The 1944 Orson Welles film explicitly declares, on screen, that the central events take place in 1839. But to the picky reader of Charlotte's novel the time scheme is a minefield. All over the place. When, for example, she recalls her journey from France (a few months before Jane's arrival at Thornfield) Adèle describes 'a great ship with a chimney that smoked – how it did smoke!'

Steam-driven vessels did not provide services across the

channel until well into the 1820s. But if smoky ships are momen-
tarily glimpsed (or smelled) in *Jane Eyre*, steam-engined trains
are wholly absent. That reinforces a mid-1820s, not 1830s date.
Since the epilogue is set ten years on, it is feasible that Mr and
Mrs Rochester the second, and their offspring the first, might
travel on Mr Stephenson's wonderful new transport system (as
did Anne Brontë, on her last journey, to Scarborough, and her
final station in life).

There is a problem, however, with *Jane Eyre*'s mid-1820s setting. It clashes with the clearest date-marker in the narrative,
inserted with some care by Brontë, it seems. Late in the novel,
Jane has settled in with St John Rivers and his sisters and is
installed professionally as a teacher at Morton School.

On 5 November (an anti-Papist holiday) St John brings
Jane 'a book for evening solace' as she is amusing herself
sketching (the day's darning and Bible-reading has been done,
presumably):

> he laid on the table a new publication – a poem: one
> of those genuine productions so often vouchsafed to
> the fortunate public of those days – the golden age of
> modern literature. Alas! the readers of our era are less
> favoured. But courage! I will not pause either to accuse
> or repine. I know poetry is not dead, nor genius lost;
> nor has Mammon gained power over either, to bind or
> slay: they will both assert their existence, their presence,
> their liberty and strength again one day. Powerful angels,
> safe in heaven! they smile when sordid souls triumph,
> and feeble ones weep over their destruction. Poetry
> destroyed? Genius banished? No! Mediocrity, no: do
> not let envy prompt you to the thought. No; they not

only live, but reign and redeem: and without their divine
influence spread everywhere, you would be in hell – the
hell of your own meanness.

While I was eagerly glancing at the bright pages of
'Marmion' (for 'Marmion' it was), St. John stooped to
examine my drawing.

It's a 'new poem', we're told.

Scott's long narrative poem *Marmion* was published in late
February 1808 as a book, by Archibald Constable. This, clearly
is what St John Rivers (hoping against hope to win Jane) has
purchased (it cost a whopping guinea – he was splashing out).

But 1808 makes nonsense of critical elements in the characters' prehistories. It would give Jane, for example, a birth date of
1777. More importantly the novel does not 'feel' as if were taking
place in the first, pre-Regency, decade of the 19th century. Smoky
chimney stacks on cross-channel steamers seem more apropos.
The Orson Welles 1839 Victorian setting, if only one could justify
it by internal evidence, seems more right. But one can't get far
beyond 'seems'. One has to conclude that dates are slippery in
Jane Eyre and not worry too much about them.

In stark contrast *Wuthering Heights* has an internal time
scheme as precisely laid out as the *Annual Register*. The tight-
ness of the chronology was first tabulated, and discussed, by
C.P. Sanger, in an influential essay, in 1926. By reference to
Sanger's table one can draw up, for example, a births, marriages
and deaths list. This is how such a list opens:

1757, June: Hindley Earnshaw born
1757, August: Ellen Dean born
1762, January: Edgar Linton born

1764, July: Heathcliff born
1765, May: Catherine Earnshaw born
1765, October: Isabella Linton born
1773, May: Mrs Earnshaw dies
1777, October: Mr Earnshaw dies
1778, June: Hareton Earnshaw is born
1778, September: Frances dies

And so on and so on until Lockwood's last visit to Wuthering Heights, in September 1802, and Cathy's marriage to Hareton the January following. One can trace every event in the novel with this eerie chronological exactitude. If you are interested in doing so, do what I did for the above, type 'Wuthering Heights Sanger Timeline' into a search engine and take it from there.

I know of no other work of Victorian fiction where you can do this. Or, to be honest, would want to. Nor does C.P. Sanger. 'In actual life,' he says:

> I have never come across a pedigree of such absolute symmetry [...]. It is a remarkable piece of symmetry in a tempestuous book.

What keeps *Wuthering Heights* completely watertight, as regards dates, is that Emily Brontë does not refer to a single external historicising event. The American War of Independence, the Napoleonic Wars, the madness of King George? Unworthy of mention. There is no larger historical framework around the micro-history of the Heights. The self-enclosure is, when one ruminates on it, disturbing, verging as it does on a kind of historical solipsism. There is something creatively neurotic about it.

ELEMENTARY

It was David Lodge, I think, who first drew attention to Charlotte
Brontë's fondness for 'elemental' names, in *Jane Eyre*.* They are
clearly meaningful, but sometimes the intended meaning is less
than clear. Nonetheless, Lodge is convincing on his fellow novelist's play with 'air' – Ariel-like spirituality, which infuses the
character of the heroine called 'Eyre'. She soars, like an eagle,
to its airy 'eyrie'. One can easily get carried away into ever more
ingenious connections.

So too one can decode the name of the smoulderingly resent-
ful Helen Burns, Jane's bosom companion at Lowood ('Low
Wood', NB), whose rebellion is extinguished into self-destroying
masochism by the evangelical Miss Temple (one could work, of
course, on that name). Her (head)master is Mr Brocklehurst.
Charlotte knew northern dialect well enough to realise that
meant 'the wood which smells of fart'. One suspects she intended
that under-meaning.

'Burn' connotes, simultaneously, flame and water (as in the
Yorkshire dialect burn = brook). Another watery character, the
sluggish St John Rivers can never – slow-flowing water that he
is – be a mate for Jane, the airy one. But 'St John', pronounced
'Sinjin' has the faintest overtone of 'singeing'. Water that burns.

Dismantling the elemental ingredients of Brontëan names
would be an interesting litcrit parlour game (Lodge, one recalls,
is the inventor of the wittiest of such games, 'Humiliation', in
which the winner is the academic who can come up with the most
flagrantly embarrassing work of fiction he/she has never read).

* In *The Language of Fiction*, 1967.

Who, from the top of their head (no recourse to Wikicribs), can come up with the best list? Here's mine – some may be less than elemental; all, however, are interestingly allusive:

Heathcliff – easy: heath and cliff.

Earnshaw – less easy. It's dialect etymology is 'eyrie of eagles'.

Linton – flax-town (a clue as to where the *nouveau riche* family's wealth has come from).

Lockwood – life for him is full of doors he will never go through.

Gérard Moore (*Shirley*) – another easy hit. 'Gérard', though, is, etymologically, 'brave'.

Lucy Snowe (*Villette*) – light ('lux') and snow. When not high on opium, Miss Snowe is the coldest of the Brontë heroines.

Wildfell Hall – savage valley. And short for 'wild fell(ow)', which is what Arthur Huntingdon is.

Northangerland (Branwell's favourite pseudonym) – 'anger of the north'.

Thrushcross Grange – crucified songbird.

Caroline Helstone (*Shirley*) – hailstones.

Shirley Keeldar (*Shirley*) – very remote. Keeldar was the name of a stone which Northumbrian chiefs passed by on their installation ceremony.

A second parlour game suggests itself. What are these elemental/cosmic names (or the particles within them) doing in the Brontëan *gesamtwerk*? How should the reader put them to interpretative use? Have no fear, academic ingenuity will find a use in any number of articles in learned journals and PhD theses.

EXTRADIEGESIS

The 1950s had its irony-hunting 'deep readers' (see below, 'Villainy', page 180). The 1970s and after had its 'theorists'. Intradiegesis and extradiegesis were two tools the theorists put in the literary toolkit. What are they? The easiest example is the most dramatic extradiegetic remark in Victorian fiction:

Reader, I married him.

The remark breaks out of the 'design' (diegesis) of the novel – tramples through the convention of narrator–narratee which we observe. We, the reader, are not there. It is an extradiegetic moment. When, a line or two later, she says to her cook, 'Mary, I have been married to Mr. Rochester this morning', it is intradiegetic. Contained within the novel's design (diegesis).

This big word may or may not be found useful. What feminist critics note (feminism was another of the doctrines riding high in the 1970s and after) is the transitive construction. 'I married him' – not 'we got married' or, heaven forfend, 'he married me'. The simple sentence conveys the all-important fact: Jane is 'empowered'. This is the woman who saved him on their first meeting, when he fell off his horse, who saved him from burning to death in his bed and who, finally, chose him as her mate.

FLOSSY

There is an oddity in the late correspondence of Patrick Brontë, when he writes a light-hearted letter to Charlotte in the person of 'Flossy'. It was obviously a regular game between them.

Flossy was a black and white Cavalier King Charles spaniel (no ordinary hound), given to Anne, as a puppy, by her Robinson pupils at Thorp Green, in 1843. It was a perfect gift for her. Flossy became a thing Anne loved – more than she loved most of humanity, who, as she wrote in her prayer book after witnessing the shenanigans (most painfully her brother's adulteries) at Thorpe Green, 'disgusted' her.

Dogs mattered in Haworth, channelling, as the animals do, warmer emotions than family members could openly express to each other. Luckily most dogs are very sensible about this. Flossy was stroked and pampered. There are complaints, late in her life, that she is getting too fat. There was not a lot of obesity at Haworth.

In her youth, she was given to sheep-worrying. She littered (who the male dog was is not recorded – a thoroughbred, one hopes). A puppy was passed on to Ellen Nussey, Charlotte's close friend. It, too, was called Flossy. The dog was, one senses, much cuddled and its silky fur was a pleasure to the stroking hand. Flossy (transmuted into a wire-haired terrier) had a lead role, as 'Snap', in *Agnes Grey*. Snap it is who eventually brings together Weston and the heroine in what will be a happy marriage.

Flossy had privileges denied the other Haworth dogs (there were many). Look, for example, at the picture overleaf – from one of the few surviving pages of Emily's diaries.

What is interesting is that Flossy is on Emily's bed (it is, inspection reveals, a 'closet' bed, like that which Lockwood sleeps in at Wuthering Heights – another fact worth noting). But Emily is serenely ignoring him. When Keeper dared lie on her bed the beast was thrashed and punched. Note that Keeper is lying dutifully at his mistress's feet. Good, good dog, one mutters.

A sketch in Emily's diary, showing Emily, Keeper and Flossy.

Emily's last recorded act, the night before she died, was to feed Flossy. Overfeed her, perhaps.

After Anne died (Flossy did not, apparently, accompany his mistress to Scarborough, on her last pilgrimage) she was looked after by Charlotte who was, we are told, less of a dog-lover, and probably more of a cat person than her sisters. Charlotte noted that all her life, Flossy seemed to be waiting for Anne's return (as Keeper pined and whined for dead Emily).

Flossy died, full of years, in 1854, having outlived virtually all the family. We are told she expired, aged eleven (77 in dog years) 'without a pang'. Would that her owner had been as lucky.*

* There is some dispute about details of Flossy – even her/his sex. I have taken the above details from the resourceful Belgian Brontëans at kleurrijkBrontësisters.blogspot.co.uk

GHOSTS

'Besides this earth, and besides the race of men, there is an invisible world and a kingdom of spirits: that world is round us, for it is everywhere …'

So says Helen Burns in *Jane Eyre*. Confirmation of this spectral circumambience is found everywhere in the Brontë world. There is a legend that Emily, then three years old, was placed, for household convenience, in the bedroom where her mother, who had barely finished nursing her, lay as a corpse (where else to put a small child, with the gloomy bustle of 'undertaking' going on?).

If, as one can easily picture, the little girl looked across the room, her little mind must have been unable to ascertain whether the person on the bed were sleeping or awake – or something in between.

Lifelong belief in ghosts is sown deep in childhood. It was Robert Louis Stevenson's night-nurse, Cummy, who chilled the little fellow's spine with the bedtime tales which would flower as *Dr Jekyll and Mr Hyde* and a volume's worth of the finest Victorian ghost stories.

Tabitha Aykroyd came as housekeeper to Haworth aged 53, initially as a nurse, when all the longer-living sisters were under eight. Tabby, like all her generation and class, believed in 'fairies'. 'It wur the factories,' she believed, 'as had driven them away!'

Supernaturalism is rife in the Angria/Gondal sagas. A classic piece of juvenilia from Charlotte, 'Napoleon and the Spectre', was written in 1833, when she was seventeen. It's a ghost story worthy of Poe. Read it.

But, as Charlotte put it, the novels she wrote for the world at large, as 'Currer Bell', beginning with *The Professor*, inhabit a world as real 'as Monday morning'. She was a reformed author. So, too, was Anne. And Emily? Not so reformed.

The reader may be led to believe that there is a night-time ghost, bent on revenge, at Thornton Hall. But it is revealed to be the all-too-real arsonist Bertha. Lucy Snowe has hallucinatory visions, but they are opium-induced. Blame the apothecary. Delirium tremens torments Arthur Huntington with terrifying visions in *The Tenant of Wildfell Hall*. But they are the product of bottles, not the world beyond the veil. Blame those who supplied him with gin.

Emily alone gives any credence to the actual existence of ghosts, working them into the fabric of her narrative. She turns the screw delicately. Screw-turning is Henry James's term for the one thing a ghost story needs. A gentle hand, gradually pulling the reader in.

The word 'ghost(s)' surfaces eleven times in the text of *Wuthering Heights* – usually with the implication that they are as real as all the others in the house. It is strongly suggested that the two main characters live on, after burial, as ghosts. When Cathy dies, Heathcliff 'vociferates' (as Emily likes to put it), with a dreadful oath: 'I know that ghosts have wandered on earth. Be with me always – take any form – drive me mad!' She obliges.

Cathy's first appearance in the novel is as the spectre scrabbling at the window pane. The last appearance of Heathcliff is one of the finest ghost scenes in Victorian literature – worthy of M.R. James. Lockwood has returned to Wuthering Heights. It is summer: flowers bloom; wedding bells are imminent, as is a general removal to civilised Thrushcross. Heathcliff is dead and gone, the world reassures itself. Nelly is a happy woman. But, as she confides, uneasily, to her erstwhile employer Lockwood:

the country folks, if you ask them, would swear on the Bible that he *walks*: there are those who speak to having met him near the church, and on the moor, and even within this house. Idle tales, you'll say, and so say I. Yet that old man by the kitchen fire affirms he has seen two on 'em looking out of his chamber window on every rainy night since his death: – and an odd thing happened to me about a month ago. I was going to the Grange one evening – a dark evening, threatening thunder – and, just at the turn of the Heights, I encountered a little boy with a sheep and two lambs before him; he was crying terribly; and I supposed the lambs were skittish, and would not be guided.

'What is the matter, my little man?' I asked.

'There's Heathcliff and a woman yonder, under t' nab,' he blubbered, 'un' I darnut pass 'em.'

I saw nothing; but neither the sheep nor he would go on so I bid him take the road lower down. He probably raised the phantoms from thinking, as he traversed the moors alone, on the nonsense he had heard his parents and companions repeat. Yet, still, I don't like being out in the dark now; and I don't like being left by myself in this grim house: I cannot help it.

The nervous sheep are a fine touch. They *know*. Baa!

Lockwood goes himself to look at the graves, in the now decayed churchyard. Are they sleeping? Or are they – horrible thought – still writhingly alive? One recalls (fancifully, I grant) three-year-old Emily looking at her mother. Alive, or dead, or something in between?

GRACE

In defence of Mrs Poole, drunken gaoler

Grace Poole is an 'upper servant' – a 'keeper of the keys', like Esther Summerson in *Bleak House*. The upperness is indicated by the fact she has a surname. Lower servants were so many Abigails and Jameses.

But unlike Dickens's incomparable Esther, Grace is a catastrophically incompetent keeper of the keys, allowing her charge, the demented Bertha, to break out and commit arson – not just once, but twice. The second time the first Mrs Rochester falls on the household like a plague of Egypt. She plunges (or is thrown – see below, 'Murder?', page 105) to her death exulting in the destruction of Thornfield Hall, Rochester's eyeballs, and one of his arms.

Some have assumed Mrs Poole is based on Martha Wright, the servant who attended Patrick's wife Maria in her last illness. The family, for unspecified reasons, felt obliged to dismiss her. She got her own back by recounting some juicy stories to Mrs Gaskell. Juliet Barker shrewdly guesses that, like Grace Poole, Martha had a weakness for the bottle. It could also have been that, as a trained nurse not a skivvy, her wages were too high for her to be kept on (although there was always some sick person to nurse at the parsonage). One of the few things one is told about Mrs Poole is that her wages are strangely high. Jane wonders about that.

There's no Black Bull in the vicinity of Thornfield (as there was for Branwell's convenience at the parsonage) and the assumption is that her gin bottle is replenished by her son, her assistant in the round-the-clock attendance Bertha requires.

Grace Poole inspires some interesting speculations about 'care'. The Brontës were interested in lunacy and madness. They were not, Mrs Gaskell's version of the family history reminds us, ignorant of what it was to have deranged relatives in the house. Patrick was eccentric and in less loving families Branwell might well have found himself institutionalised when out of his mind.

The hothouse decade in which the sisters were writing their six mature novels saw huge reforms in the treatment of the mentally infirm. The madhouse was transforming itself into the modern lunatic asylum (the word comes from the Greek for 'shelter').

The pioneer physician in this transformation was John Conolly (1794–1866). Conolly advocated radical change in the restraint of lunatics, drawing on the example of the Quaker retreats, where the mad were treated with gentleness. It was, these retreats demonstrated, therapy more successful than the whip.

In 1839 Conolly was appointed governor at Hanwell, the leading asylum in the country, serving greater London. With maximum publicity (he was an inveterate self-advertiser) he inaugurated a policy of humane reform. He abolished the panoply of straitjackets, manacles and whips by which the inmates had traditionally been regulated. Institutionalisation was a necessary evil. But Conolly believed the best care of the deranged was in 'home care'.

Dickens was an early admirer of Conolly. Mr Dick, in *David Copperfield*, and Betsey Trotwood's indulgent care for him at home is a florid Dickensian tribute to Conolly's non-restraint system. Miss Trotwood rescued Mr Dick from a madhouse, whose gothic horrors are hinted at. He blooms, under her kindness, into the most amiable of maniacs, in his kite flying and obsession with King Charles's head.

Jane Eyre suggests that Charlotte had, like Dickens, thought about the proper treatment of the insane – more particularly the question of restraint versus non-restraint. In describing to Jane his decision to keep Bertha at home (he could very easily have found some amenable madhouse to incarcerate her) Rochester, rather surprisingly, reveals himself to be a strong proponent of the non-restraint doctrine.

He recruited, he divulges, Mrs Poole and her son, at considerable expense, from the 'Grimsby Retreat' where both previously worked and Poole Jnr occupied a senior position as keeper. The term 'retreat' makes clear that Rochester adheres to the system successfully pioneered by the Quakers at their famous 'York Retreat' (headed by the heroic Henry Tuke) in the late 18th century. It inspired Conolly's reforms. It is equally clear that, in her attic, Bertha is held in a minimum-security environment except when she is, as Mrs Poole puts it, 'rageous'. Or, alas, when Mrs Poole is pissed out of her mind.

GUADELOUPE

Villette has a famously teasing double ending: Paul Emanuel, the 'master', may come back from distant parts to make Lucy his bride, enriched, and able to set up their own school. Happy ever after. Or Paul may drown in one of the storms, on whose gusts banshees ride. Lucy Snowe is eloquent on the subject of banshees – Irish ghouls. She fears them when the wind rises.

Her *maître* has gone to the French West Indies, specifically the protectorate Guadeloupe, for a three-year tour. As Lucy informs us, bluntly, 'Its alpha is Mammon and its omega Interest'. Money, sucked out of the plantations, via slave labour, she means. Mme Walravens has a large estate in Basseterre: sugar (for rum) would be its main crop. Black slaves are Guadeloupe's workforce. The owner has asked Paul Emanuel to be her 'competent' agent.

If 'duly looked after' the estate will be 'largely productive'. Paul will, himself, profit handsomely. Mammon, Mammon, Mammon.

Ostensibly (and unconvincingly) he goes to the West Indies (leaving Lucy behind) from a sense of duty. 'No living being,' says Lucy, loyally, 'ever humbly laid his advantage at M. Emanuel's feet, or confidingly put it into his hands, that he spurned the trust, or repulsed the repository.'

Whatever might be Paul's 'private pain or inward reluctance to leave Europe', he accedes to Mme Walravens's request. It is, one might think, strange that Paul should accede. The claims of Lucy and his own happiness would seem to be stronger than the financial convenience of Madame Walravens.

Even more oddly, Paul Emanuel is not a businessman, but a schoolteacher. Of girls. The professor is, however, notorious for 'discipline'. It is not hard to deduce what duties are required from a 'competent' agent in Guadeloupe at this period. Simon Legree, the villainous overseer in *Uncle Tom's Cabin*, would fit the bill.

The date of *Villette's* action is the early 1840s: more or less the period of Charlotte's own fraught residence in Brussels and tutelage there by her own *maître*, Constantin Héger (see below, 'Letters', page 75). Slavery had finally been abolished in the British West Indies in 1833, precipitating a disastrous slump in the islands' sugar industry, with the widespread defection of pressed (enslaved) labour from the plantations into idle destitution. Hard days for absentee owners.

In colonial Guadeloupe, under the unenlightened French imperial regime, the institution of slavery (and the profitability of the sugar plantations) was to limp along until its long overdue abolition in 1848.

The stern and dictatorial Professor Paul Emanuel – the Napoleon of Mme Beck's classroom – has clearly been recruited to rally the increasingly dissident labourers of Madame Walraverns' estate, with whips and scorpions if necessary. They will have picked up rumours about emancipation and will be a surly and rebellious crew.

For 'competent', then, read 'brutal'. For 'Paul Emanuel' read 'Kurtz' (another Belgian, as it happens). For 'Guadeloupe' read 'Heart of Darkness'.

There is another putative factor in the virtuous Mme Walravens choosing Paul Emanuel as her overseer. He has shown himself, in his attendance at Mme Beck's establishment, remarkably capable of restraining himself, sexually, in the presence of nubile young women (and, of course, Mme Beck herself). Even Lucy, who would give herself as willingly as, we surmise, Charlotte would have given herself to Héger, is safe. Jezebel and Salome would fail with Paul Emanuel. He could resist even the fall of the seventh veil.

Sexual restraint will be imperative when Paul takes up his new post. All 19th-century accounts of Guadeloupe stress that it is a place of irresistible temptation for European males. As the fourteenth edition of the *Encyclopaedia Britannica* coyly records:

> Guadeloupe has a few white officials and planters, a few East Indian immigrants from the French possessions in India, and the rest negroes and mulattoes. These are famous for their grace and beauty of both form and feature. Women greatly outnumber men and illegitimate births are very numerous.

Many of those births, one can suspect, are of mixed race. Clearly only a man of iron self-discipline can be trusted to remain celibate three hot years in such a Sodom, keeping himself pure for his true love across the seas. A man, that is, such as Paul Emanuel. The maître.

HANDS

Recently the admirable novelist, and Brontë lover, Polly Samson texted to ask about the following puzzle she had noted in *Jane Eyre*. We are told when Jane and Edward are happily settled that his 'left arm, the mutilated one, he kept hidden in his bosom'. Like Nelson and his mutilated right arm.

But, later on, Jane Rochester (as she now is) informs us:

> Mr. Rochester continued blind the first two years of our union: perhaps it was that circumstance that drew us so very near – that knit us so very close! for I was then his vision, as I am still his right hand.

So which of his hands did he lose, on the night he was rid (one way or another – see below, 'Murder?', page 105) of the first Mrs Rochester? It's a teasing conundrum. It could, of course, be a simple error. But the book was proofed carefully in Smith, Elder's office and such an obvious mistake would have been picked up. There must be a subtler explanation.

The best answer I could come up with for Polly Samson was as follows. I think the 'right hand' reference is not physiological but religiously metaphorical, and not to be taken literally. Charlotte was saturated in the Bible. The daughter of a clergyman, later the wife of a clergyman, she attended church, listened to morning and evening home prayers, all her life. She probably dreamed in KJV English.

As the Bible tells us, God is right-handed. There are many references: viz, the following from Ephesians 1:19–21.

> [19]And what is the exceeding greatness of his power to us-ward who believe, according to the working of his mighty power, [20]Which he wrought in Christ, when he raised him from the dead, *and set him at his own right hand* in the heavenly places, [my italics] [21]Far above all principality, and power, and might, and dominion, and every name that is named, not only in this world, but also in that which is to come.

I suspect what the left/right-hand switch means is that, in marriage, Charlotte supplies – or, at least shares – her master's lost male power. No error, but something of a complacent wifely boast. Nothing sinister in the Rochesters' (second) marriage. The first? Don't ask.

THE HOUND OF HAWORTH

One of the few things we know Emily to have said in her short life was to her class in Belgium. She informed her charges, contemptuously, that when it came to animals, she loved her dog more than she loved beastly them.

Love her dog she certainly did – in fact more, perhaps, than the whole human race. But Emily Brontë would not be an automatic candidate for the Paul O'Grady Prize for Kindness to Our Four-legged Friends. Of the few acts we know her to have committed in life, other than writing a wonderful novel, many of them centre on dogs and her sometimes questionable treatment of them.

All the sisters seem to have been fond of domestic animals. With Emily, it went further. As Mrs Gaskell records:

> Some one speaking of her to me ... said, 'she never showed regard to any human creature; all her love was reserved for animals.'

'All'? It seems, somehow, 'inhuman'. Gaskell goes on to moralise:

> The helplessness of an animal was its passport to Charlotte's heart; the fierce, wild intractability of its nature was what often recommended it to Emily.

There is subliminal hint of quasi-sexual relationship lurking in Gaskell's description. Emily's 'love', one notes, was reserved, exclusively, for the male of the canine species. Charlotte Brontë reproduced in *Shirley*, 'Emily's way of sitting on the rug reading, with her arm round her rough bull-dog's neck'. The bulldog in the novel, 'Tartar', is a mirror image of Emily's dog, Keeper. The intercourse on the floor is given with the full blast of Charlottian floridity, veering just on the edge of eroticism:

> The tawny and lionlike bulk of Tartar is ever stretched beside her, his negro muzzle laid on his fore paws – straight, strong, and shapely as the limbs of an Alpine wolf. One hand of the mistress generally reposes on the loving serf's rude head, because if she takes it away he groans and is discontented.

Mrs Gaskell (having heard it from Charlotte) retails an extraordinary anecdote, testifying to Emily's near-psychotic intrapunitiveness. A strange dog ran past the parsonage, 'with hanging head and lolling tongue'. Emily gave it 'a merciful draught of water'. It gave her in return, a 'maddened snap'. Rabid! Rushing downstairs into the kitchen Emily took up one of Tabby's red-hot 'Italian irons' and 'seared' the wound. She told no one, until much later, to forestall 'the terrors that might beset their weaker minds'.

That event, too, is reproduced in *Shirley*. It's odd. It would have been more prosocial to put out a warning to the community: 'Beware! Rabid dog on loose'. Or to have called on the Revd Brontë to dispatch the diseased beast with his trusty pistol (as does Atticus Finch, pro bono publico, in *To Kill a Mockingbird*).

Emily's was the usual remedy for being bitten by a rabid animal – usually canine. And Yorkshire was where, in England, it most often happened. Neil Pemberton, in the delightfully titled *Mad Dogs and Englishmen*, tells us:

> The idea of being bitten, the fear of being bitten or being approached by a stray dog was pretty much present and persistent, and it was particularly potent in a place like Bradford. Rabies was seen as a disease of the North: Lancashire and the West Riding were seen as the rabies capitals.

Until Pasteur's vaccine, late in the century, immediate cauterisation was the only remedy (it did not bring immediate relief: the horrific disease could wait a year to present itself).

Emily's 'love' of dogs went along with a fascinated respect for the violence and danger they embodied. One recalls, in *Wuthering Heights*, Catherine's being mauled by one of the four-legged keepers at Thrushcross Grange. It imbues in Heathcliff a lifelong

Emily, from an incomplete painting by Branwell.

hatred of dogs. He pauses, in eloping with Isabella, to strangle
her pet. 'I wink to see my father strike a dog,' says his son, 'he
does it so hard.'

Emily's Keeper was given as a gift – from whom is not known
– and was not a friendly beast. Keeper, we are told:

> was faithful to the depths of his nature as long as he was
> with friends; but he who struck him with a stick or whip,
> roused the relentless nature of the brute, who flew at his
> throat forthwith, and held him there till one or the other
> was at the point of death.

Again via Charlotte, Mrs Gaskell puts on record a vivid anecdote.
Keeper loved to lie on his mistress's bed 'in drowsy voluptuous-
ness', soiling its cleanliness. In the 'gathering dusk of an autumn
evening', Emily was informed by Tabby that, despite numerous
prohibitions and beatings, he had done it again.

> Charlotte saw Emily's whitening face, and set mouth, but
> dared not speak to interfere; no one dared when Emily's
> eyes glowed in that manner out of the paleness of her
> face, and when her lips were so compressed into stone.

As the shadows of night fell, she dragged the growling beast
downstairs by the 'scuff of his neck'. If she let him go, he might
go for her throat. She had no hand free to get a stick. Instead,
she punched Keeper mercilessly in his 'red fierce eyes' until he was
half-blind, and thoroughly 'mastered'. The generous dog, Gaskell
tells us 'owed her no grudge; he loved her dearly ever after; he
walked first among the mourners to her funeral; he slept moan-
ing for nights at the door of her empty room.' Her demon lover.

IDIOT CHILD

Such was Charlotte's rueful name for her first novel, *The Professor* (originally *The Master*). It suffered nine rejections, six under the authorial name 'Currer Bell'. Even the bestselling author of *Jane Eyre* could not prevail on the friendliest of publishers, George Smith, to put *The Professor* into print, in the years of her fame.

The story is easily summarised, as are its springs of creation. *The Professor* was written (most likely) in autumn 1844, after Charlotte's return from Brussels and in the furnace-like emotions her stay there had kindled. This was the city where she found love, in her hopeless infatuation with her professor (or *maître/ master*), the unassailably virtuous (and married) M. Héger. A man who could have changed the whole course of Victorian fiction with a marital slip.

In terms of her artistic development, *The Professor* represents Charlotte's departure from the fantasy world of Gondal/Angria for the real world – a world as real 'as Monday morning'.

The novel is narrated autobiographically by William Crimsworth. The setting is loosely late 1830s. The hero is an Etonian in his early twenties (a genus Charlotte Brontë knew less well than she did the man in the moon). William is orphaned and unless he wants to marry a flibbertigibbet cousin (much of the novel is taken up with his distaste for flibbertigibbets) he must work. He accepts the curse stoically.

He enrols as a £90 p.a. clerk for his rich, northern mill-owner brother Edward. They have been alienated for years (the family background is complex and somewhat blurred). A bully and self-made man, Edward despises 'soft' southrons like William. But if there is one thing an Etonian knows it is how to face down bullies. After a horsewhipping fracas and with the assistance of a friendly 'radical' mill-owner, Yorke Hunsden, William takes off for Brussels, to teach English in a boarding school.

The proprietress of a neighbouring girls' school, Zoraïde Reuter, a Catholic as sirenic as her name, lures William, sexually. But he sees through her wiles in favour of a Protestant pupil, Frances Henri, a demure young Anglo-Swiss. Like himself she is a *fillette* of impeccable earnestness. They marry, set up their own school, and have children (authorial wish-fulfilment run riot).

On the edge of the couple's terminal 'happy ever after', the brutal Edward, enriched by 'steam', carries on prosecuting the industrial revolution, turning the West Ridings into a wasteland.

Famously, George Smith, Charlotte's publishing saviour, and his adviser William Smith Williams, saw 'something' in the book when the elsewhere rejected manuscript was submitted to them by 'Mr Bell'. Williams, particularly, is one of the unsung heroes of Victorian fiction.

Smith Elder rejected the manuscript but commissioned a three-decker (*The Professor* would have made up a meagre two volumes: generally disliked by circulating libraries – see below, 'Three-Decker', page 162). The three-decker arrived at their office a few months later as *Jane Eyre*. In it the idea of the 'master' (Jane's term of address to Rochester, even after marriage) is let rip. There are other 'seeds' in *The Professor*, which would later bloom. The *Villette* love-in-a-classroom story is embryonically there. There are moments in the first third of the novel, in the clash between William and Edward, when we glimpse the skeletal outline of an unwritten 'social problem' ('factory') novel of the *North and South* or *Hard Times* kind. Charlotte would pursue that theme in *Shirley*.

There are other moments in *The Professor* when one feels a

wholly different novel struggling to get out. William gives Frances a *devoir* (assignment). She is instructed to write an essay on Alfred, the peasant's cottage, and the burnt cakes. This is what Frances (one can assume it's a version of Charlotte, writing to impress Héger) comes up with:

> Take care, young man [commands the peasant wife], that you fasten the door well … whatever sound you hear stir not and look not out. The night will soon fall … strange noises are often heard … you might chance to hear, as it were, a child cry, and on opening the door to give it succour … a shadowy goblin dog might rush over the threshold; or more awful still, if something flapped, as with wings, against the lattice, and then a raven or a white dove flew in and settled on the hearth, such a visitor would be a sure sign of misfortune. The stranger, left alone, listens awhile to the muffled snow-wind.

The real world of Monday morning seems to have slipped a bit and a strong whiff of – what else? – *Wuthering Heights* assails the reader's nostrils. There would be no readers, alas, of Charlotte's idiot child to be assailed by this whiff until well after its fond mother's death.

THE IDIOT CHILD AND ME

The Professor was the first Brontë novel I read. My well-meaning mother, discerning, perhaps, an academic future for her child, gave me a second-hand copy. (There was, I was often told, a 'clairvoyant' gift in my family. My grandmother was a tassologist of renown in Colchester, widely consulted. No tea leaf held its secrets from Daisy Salter.)

The book my mother put my way – God knows where she got it – was a treasure (although it would be four years before I went on to *Wuthering Heights*). It was, I now know, the mass-market Dent 1905 edition of *The Professor*. What distinguished it were the six full-page, colour-processed pictures by Edmund Dulac – the finest artist, for my money, ever to have illustrated the Brontë works (Charlotte prohibited illustration of her novels during her lifetime; her sisters, dealing with a lower class of publisher, were never asked).

Dulac had emigrated as a young man to London from Paris. Aged a mere 22, he was recruited by Dent to illustrate a collected Brontë edition, using the new technologies for coloured reproduction pioneered in the London book world (one of the reasons Edmund had emigrated).

I was a lonely little boy, eleven years old. Most of the story flew over my head. But I recall, to this day, the impact on me of one of Dulac's illustrations, featuring a pensive young William Crimsworth overlooking an industrial townscape a short distance away. The caption reads: 'Steam, trade, machinery had long banished from it all romance and seclusion'.

It represents what is a moment of truth for William. He is at the turning point of his life. Is he about to become part of the system's 'machinery'? 'Muck and brass', as the phrase went? The relevant passage in the book reads:

> At a distance of five miles, a valley, opening between the low hills, held in its cups the great town of X——. A dense, permanent vapour brooded over this locality – there lay Edward's 'Concern'. I forced my eye to scrutinise

this prospect, I forced my mind to dwell on it for a time, and when I found that it communicated no pleasurable emotion to my heart — that it stirred in me none of the hopes a man ought to feel, when he sees laid before him the scene of his life's career — I said to myself, 'William, you are a rebel against circumstances; you are a fool, and know not what you want; you have chosen trade and you shall be a tradesman …'

At this period of my life (I have written about it)* I, like William Crimsworth, was at a crux in my life. I had overheard my mother say that if I failed the eleven-plus (which I nearly did) the best thing would be for me to be apprenticed to a bricklayer (they were making good money in the late 1940s). Not quite the same downfall as an Etonian becoming a 'tradesman', but analogous to my young mind. And touched by that fine picture of Crimsworth looking at a future he does not want but cannot, perhaps, avoid.

George Smith and W.S. Williams saw 'something' in Charlotte Brontë's 'Idiot Child'. So did childish I. I still do.

JANE! JANE! JANE!

Rochester's astral telephony with Jane, precipitating their reunion and eventual marriage is one of the stranger lapses from 'Monday morning' realism which Charlotte liked to protest was the foundation of her mature fiction.

Just what day of weekly reality is this scene set in? Are we, the reader may well ask, back in Angria? Fantasy Brontëland?

* See *The Boy who Loved Books* (2009).

The situation in the narrative is as follows. Jane is at the St John Rivers home, after evening prayers. It is around nine o'clock on Monday evening.

Never a lively place, this is a very quiet moment in the parlour. Family and servants have gone to bed, St John Rivers is alone with Jane. He solemnly renews his proposal of marriage. She wavers: 'I could decide if I were but certain … were I but convinced that it is God's will I should marry you …'

Jane needs a sign from above. Little conversation is recorded, but the two are evidently together for a few hours. She, all the while, is staring, steadfastly, at the 'one candle' illuminating the room (the St John household is frugal). It gutters. As Jane describes it:

All the house was still; for I believe all, except St John and myself, were now retired to rest. The one candle was dying out: the room was full of moonlight. My heart beat fast and thick: I heard its throb.

Suddenly it stood still to an inexpressible feeling that thrilled it through, and passed at once to my head and extremities. The feeling was not like an electric shock, but it was quite as sharp, as strange, as startling: it acted on my senses as if their utmost activity hitherto had been but torpor, from which they were now summoned and forced to wake.

They rose expectant: eye and ear waited while the flesh quivered on my bones.

'What have you heard? What do you see?' asked St John. I saw nothing, but I heard a voice somewhere cry –

'Jane! Jane! Jane!' nothing more.

Is this, perhaps, the sign she is waiting for? God, as the hymn tells us, moves in mysterious ways and sometimes His signalling (as the Israelites discovered in the desert) can be very enigmatic.

> I might have said, 'Where is it?' for it did not seem in the room – nor in the house – nor in the garden: it did not come out of the air – nor from under the earth – nor from overhead. I had heard it – where, or whence, for ever impossible to know! And it was the voice of a human being – a known, loved, well-remembered voice – that of Edward Fairfax Rochester; and it spoke in pain and woe, wildly, eerily, urgently.
>
> 'I am coming!' I cried. 'Wait for me! Oh, I will come!'

Four days later, after her breakneck dash back to Thornfield, Rochester will tell Jane that on the Monday night in question he himself sat for some hours in his unlit room gazing, unblinkingly, at the moon through the window. Involuntarily, near midnight, he ejaculated, 'Jane! Jane! Jane!' Then, to his amazement, he heard her voice reply, audibly, 'I am coming; wait for me!'

That Rochester's communication, across many miles, was not hallucinatory was insisted on by Charlotte herself, defending the scene, which has always bothered some strict Brontëans. 'It is a *true* thing: it really happened,' she insisted. By which, it seems, she meant such a thing was scientifically possible. 'Really'?

Her defiant word 'truth' is, on the face of it, perverse. Some early reviewers apprehended that Brontë might be fantasising about the exciting new technology of telegraphy: see Jane's remark about 'electric shock'. But the 'wires', as Victorians called them, linking humanity (usually alongside railway lines), electrically, across great distance, was still in its infancy, and it was unlikely that it was much discussed over the breakfast table at Haworth.

What the Brontës would have been interested in (as they were with phrenology – see above, 'Bumps on the Head', page 35) were recent reports of mesmerism, 'animal magnetism', clairvoyance and tele-auditory communication. It is possible that Charlotte, in the Haworth Mechanics' Library, perhaps, came across the Revd Chauncey Hare Townshend's *Facts in Mesmerism, with Reasons for a Dispassionate Inquiry Into It* (London 1840). The book was published under Longman's highly respectable imprint, and was, for a while, taken seriously by the scientific community. In his book Townshend asserted:

> It has been said that persons in certain states either mesmeric or akin to the mesmeric can become aware of the thoughts of others without the usual communication of speech … But is there, it may still be asked, any one acknowledged instance in nature by which the possibility of receiving actual experiences other than by the normal inlets of sense can be demonstrated? There is.

To back up this blunt statement, Townshend cited numerous scientifically valid examples of telepathic communication. Meetings of minds, and voices, across great distances, requiring no soundwaves, riding the energy of animal magnetism.

The commonest way to produce a mesmeric state, or trance, is to look for a long period at a candle (I tried it myself, with moderate success, I recall, as a schoolboy – before finding substances that produced the necessary effect more quickly).

So that's it. The 'truth' of it. Or so a novelist up with the latest thinking on animal magnetism might think in 1847. No Monday morning transgression.

JANE'S CHANGE OF HEART

Jane rushes, post-haste, 'home' to Thornfield in the same way she left the place, unthinkingly, under the propulsion of overwhelming emotion. She left, one recalls, because her conscience would not allow her to remain as Rochester's mistress; nor did she trust herself to remain in the house a pure woman, Bertha raving by night upstairs.

Now that Edward has summoned her in this unusual manner (see above, 'Jane! Jane! Jane!', page 71), it seems that she does want just that. Impurity. Why else would she go back to Thornfield? She does not at this point know, living as she has been out of the way with the Riverses, that the first Mrs Rochester has conveniently committed suttee, leaving her post vacant.

Rather adultery with her 'master', Jane has evidently resolved (even though she can't consciously admit it to herself), than a lifetime of marital probity converting the Indian masses to Christianity alongside St John Rivers. Who can blame her? But what would she have done if Bertha, when she arrived home, were still in the land of the living? There is another novel there.

LETTERS

Brontë scholarship, developing at the time into outright hagiography, was turned upside down with the release, in 1913, of four surviving letters written by Charlotte to her *maître*, Constantin Héger. The letters were lucky to have survived. They had been torn up, tossed away, retrieved (by an unknown hand) and laboriously sewn together (clearly by a female hand). They give visible proof of trailing havoc and high temperature behind them. Oddly, they were used at one point to jot down shopping lists. The name of M. Héger's bootmaker has been detected. They were, nonetheless, stored in Mme Héger's jewel box. For reasons one can easily surmise, these letters were 'valuables'.

The four manuscripts were donated to the British Museum and published, in full, in *The Times*. They had been preserved in the family for decades because the Hégers (most strongly the matriarch) felt they would be needed to prove that Charlotte Brontë's passion for Constantin was a one-way thing. The patriarch of the family was unassailably virtuous – no seducer of young English *assistantes*. Not he. Here is the incontrovertible proof. Charlotte Brontë was a little English fool.

The Hégers were the family Charlotte and Emily stayed with as pupils, and undermistresses, in Brussels, on their one protracted period away from Haworth. The letters, said Héger's son Paul, had been 'religiously preserved' (apart, that is, from the tossing, sewing, and bootmaker details). They were now made public to the English nation as revealing 'what has hitherto been spoken of as the "Secret of Charlotte Brontë", and show how groundless is the suspicion which has resulted from the natural speculations of critics and biographers'.

Groundless, that is, as regards the conduct of Héger *père*, not the infatuation of deranged Mlle Brontë. Among themselves the Hégers' verdict on the besotted *anglaise* was cruel. Héger recalled 'sadly defective teeth – somewhat ill-favoured'. The women wondered how so 'ugly' a girl thought she could entice the virtuous, handsome Constantin.

The family had no reason to be kind. The depiction of Mme Beck (clearly Mme Héger), the *pensionnat* proprietor in *Villette*, was cruel. The description of the *pensionnat Beck*'s regime of 'espionage' (and the doltishness of the pupils) was defamatory, and commercially damaging. It is not hard to see the novel as the outpouring of a woman scorned (it is, of course, much more).

Worst of all, from the Hégers' aggrieved point of view, *Villette*, as the years passed, was a perennial bestseller. More and more people were reading it and drawing ill-informed conclusions about Constantin's professional conduct. The Hégers were, as the century turned, a well-known and respected family in Brussels.

Mrs Gaskell knew about the letters (she visited the Hégers while writing her biography) but suppressed any 'natural speculation' she may have felt. 'I cannot tell you how I should deprecate anything leading to the publication of these letters,' she told George Smith, the publisher of her biography, with a palpable shudder. Smith, like her, was a resolute protector of Brontë's reputation. One suspects his long suppression of *The Professor* was because of the other offensive misrepresentation of Mme Héger in that novel as the serpentine Mlle Zoraïde Reuter (one of Mme Héger's forenames was Zoe). He was more careful of Charlotte's reputation than Charlotte was.

The last straw for the Hégers was, one guesses, Clement Shorter's monumental, iconographic, *The Brontës: Life and Letters* in 1908. There was also increasing gossip (building on the love plot of *Villette*) that there must surely have been some kind of relationship beyond the strictly pedagogical between Charlotte and her professor in Brussels, when she was studying there. Trust the novel.

Not everyone did trust *Villette*. Frederika Macdonald, another English, Protestant pupil of the Hégers (fifteen years after Charlotte) was quick to defend her teachers and the family in her 1914 book entitled (echoing Paul Héger's remark) *The Secret of Charlotte Brontë*. Using the well-known rhetorical device of airing a 'false' allegation only to let it stand, Macdonald wrote:

From the moral and personal standpoint, [Charlotte Brontë] remains convicted (if she be held to be telling her own story [in *Villette*]) of the baseness of a half-confession;—and *of a dishonourable and a successful*, not a *romantic and tragical*, love for a married man. And of the treacherous wrong done a sister-woman, who threw open her home to her, when she was a friendless alien in a foreign city. And, if this were so, this traitress would have further aggravated the dishonest betrayal of her protectress, by holding up the woman she had wronged to the world's detestation, either as the contemptible and scheming Mlle. Zoraïde Reuter, of *The Professor*:—or the less contemptible but more hateful Madame Beck, in *Villette*.

Constantin Héger (1809–1896) was the husband of the proprietress, Claire, of the Héger *pensionnat* (boarding school). It catered for around 100 girls (at its fullest) in Brussels. Charlotte and Emily went there, on very generous terms, to learn French, and gain teaching experience, in 1842. A teacher of literature at a nearby boys' school, Constantin gave occasional free-ranging lessons, mainly on literature, in his wife's *pensionnat*. The couple had married in 1836, and would go on to have six children – as had

The *pensionnat* Héger

Patrick Brontë. Children, the sisters must have ruefully observed, lived longer in Brussels than Haworth.

Charlotte was at Mme Héger's establishment for two extended spells, Emily (who did not take to Brussels, missing her dog and the moors) for one year only. Héger was 33 years old when the Brontës arrived in 1842, eight years younger than his wife and six years older than Charlotte. According to Macdonald, 'Madame Héger [was] a much more attractive woman than Charlotte Brontë in so far as her personal appearance was concerned'. There are no pictures to verify this.

In *Villette* Mme Beck's 'advanced' age, is made much of:

When he was gone, Madame dropped into the chair he had just left; she rested her chin in her hand; all that was animated and amiable vanished from her face: she looked stony and stern, almost mortified and morose.

She sighed; a single, but a deep sigh. A loud bell rang for morning-school. She got up; as she passed a dressing-table with a glass upon it, she looked at her reflected image. One single white hair streaked her nut-brown tresses; she plucked it out with a shudder. In the full summer daylight, her face, though it still had the colour, could plainly be seen to have lost the texture of youth; and then, where were youth's contours? Ah, Madame! wise as you were, even *you* knew weakness.

Never had I pitied Madame before, but my heart softened towards her, when she turned darkly from the glass. A calamity had come upon her. That hag Disappointment was greeting her with a grisly 'All-hail,' and her soul rejected the intimacy.

'Hag' is hard.

A hero of the nationalist Belgian uprising of 1830 (he had fought at the barricades) Héger was, all the evidence suggests, an inspired teacher. His emotionally intense one-on-one tutorial technique anticipates what is now called 'creative writing' instruction. His two English pupils, he ordained, must copy the styles of literary masters, so as ultimately to work their way to their own style. His copyist exercises went down better with Charlotte than with Emily.

The surviving letters (all from Charlotte) were written to Héger after she left Mme Héger's *pensionnat* on New Year's Day 1844. Her stay in Brussels, and her relationship with Constantin, had been, she told her bosom friend Ellen Nussey, the biggest experience of her life.

After leaving she wrote fortnightly. Then, at Mme Héger's insistence (she evidently read the letters, with or without permission, presumably in high wifely dudgeon) it was allowed only at six-month intervals. No one knows how often Charlotte despite the prohibition wrote, what Constantin wrote (if anything) in return and how far Charlotte allowed her clearly passionate feelings to take over in letters that have not survived.

Charlotte's letters were in French: she may have felt freer to emote in that language. 'I love French for your sake with all my heart and soul,' she wrote. She only, on the evidence of her surviving correspondence, used it consistently with Constantin Héger.

The letters verge at times on the erotic – well beyond what might be expected from a grateful pupil expressing formal thanks for instruction: for example:

> Day or night I find neither rest nor peace. If I sleep I have tortured dreams in which I see you always severe, always gloomy and annoyed with me. I do not seek to justify myself, I submit to every kind of reproach – all that I know – is that I cannot – that I will not resign myself to losing the friendship of my master completely – I would rather undergo the greatest physical sufferings. If my master withdraws his friendship entirely from me I will be completely without hope … I cling on to preserving that little interest – I cling on to it as I cling on to life.

Clement Shorter's riposte on reading the letters is gallant but feeble:

> There is nothing in those letters of hers, published now for the first time, that any enthusiastic woman might not write to a man double her age, who was a married man with a family, and who had been her teacher.

The letters placed her, he nonsensically insisted, 'on a higher pedestal than ever'. Mme Héger did not perceive any pedestal. That was not why she sewed the letters up and put them in her jewel box.

Was she in love? Charlotte's pen-picture of M. Héger (in a letter to Nussey) as he first struck her in 1842 is vivid:

> He is professor of rhetoric, a man of power as to mind, but very choleric and irritable in temperament; a little black being, with a face that varies in expression. Sometimes he borrows the lineaments of an insane tom-cat, sometimes those of a delirious hyena.

The wild zoology is carried over into the first description of Paul Emanuel in *Villette*. He has, Lucy tells us, tremblingly, 'a close and picturesque resemblance to that of a black and sallow tiger'.

'Tom cat' brings with it certain implications. As does 'tiger'.* The critic Linda S. Kauffman sees in the broken flow of the surviving letters a clear-cut narrative and, possibly, the reflection of an exploitative side to Héger's pedagogy.**

The eminently level-headed Juliet Barker, having weighed all the evidence (including Héger's well-recorded 'charismatic' teaching techniques and the dangers they might represent to susceptible pupils) concludes, judiciously:

---

* In Haworth the family had two cats at the period, one called 'Tom Cat' the other 'Tiger' – neither, one guesses, judging by the names, sexually continent beasts.
** Kauffman, L. 1986, *Discourses of Desire: Gender, Genre and Epistolary Fictions*.

One cannot but feel sorry for Monsieur Héger, a married man whose character and morals were above reproach. If he replied to his highly strung former pupil, it merely encouraged her to write again. If he did not reply, in the hope that she might forget him, she brooded on his supposed neglect and became even more hysterical and obsessive.

Constantin Héger in later life, but still very much the *maître* who won Charlotte's heart.

To his credit Héger gallantly kept the embarrassing letters from public knowledge or view during his life. But he did show them to Mrs Gaskell, who could have publicised their content. Héger could have burnt them. Did he really not know his wife was fishing them out of the wastepaper basket and laboriously reassembling them to put in a safe place? The imagination strains to believe that.

One's conclusion is that Charlotte, whose experience of men was limited mainly to unattractive curates, had a 'crush' on her teacher. He may, initially, not have damped it down as a conscientious *maître* ought to have done. What flared up had a consequence that was anything but banal. Charlotte Brontë's finest novel, *Villette*, was born out of the flames of a love which could never be.

Postscript

Lyndall Gordon, a critic who has written sensitively about *l'affaire Héger*, adds a tiny (literally) additional observation to the much trawled-over manuscripts. What letters Charlotte was allowed (by Mme Héger) to write (there were surely more, outside the rules) were written in French. The language Constantin taught her, Gordon persuasively suggests, released passion the English language locked up. Nonetheless the last sentence in the batch of surviving letters is in English: 'Out of the fullness of the heart the mouth speaketh'.*

Gordon elaborates:

---

* Luke 6:45: 'A good man out of the good treasure of his heart bringeth forth that which is good; and an evil man out of the evil treasure of his heart bringeth forth that which is evil: for of the abundance of the heart his mouth speaketh.'

To bare her feelings in her own language, rooted in the eloquence of the King James Bible, touches her so strongly that she adds something which no naked eye noticed until it was blown up by a cameraman filming the letters in a small dark room at the British Library two years ago. I was reading the [English] postscript aloud and the cameraman was filming over my shoulder when suddenly he exclaimed, 'What's this?' Blown up on screen, what looked like the full stop at the end of this leave-taking turned out to be a minute heart.

This invisible message to Héger is tantamount to Mr Rochester calling to Jane across an impossible space.

In order to keep their Gondal/Angria writings from prying eyes (their disliked aunt and loved, but severe, father, specifically) the Brontë children inscribed them in microscript. This microscopy, in 1846, was drawn on as the channel for Charlotte's language of love. An emoticon, no less. A code the prying eye of needle-wielding Mme Héger could never crack.♥

LIVERPOOL

Mr Earnshaw's long walk

We are given a detailed description of how Heathcliff arrives at Wuthering Heights – the property which he will 'come into' (rather as a wolf comes into a herd of sheep).

Mr Earnshaw, a Yorkshire farmer, out of the blue announces in August 1771 that he intends to make a journey to Liverpool. The seaport lies 60 miles away (as Haworth is, by the M65, today). He will go by foot, he tells his family. He gives no explanation and it is, as far as they are aware, a spur-of-the-moment thing. There is no evidence of any letter summoning him to Liverpool.

It's very odd – and the first of a string of oddities in this primal episode in the novel. Everything thereafter will hinge on that trip to Liverpool. The first oddity is that it is 'harvest time' and good weather; no conscientious farmer would leave his crops over these days.

Mr Earnshaw says he will bring back the children presents. They will prove appropriate gifts given how their lives will turn out. Hindley demands a fiddle (he will later dissipate himself to early death); Catherine 'could ride any horse in the stable, and she chose a whip'.

Why is Mr Earnshaw making his expedition by foot? There are, as Catherine's wished-for whip indicates, horses in the stable. And there was, even at this early date, coach travel between Bradford and Liverpool. And, the biggest oddity of all, why would a Yorkshire farmer, of modest means, have to go to Liverpool in the first place? It's not a market town.

Nonetheless, Mr Earnshaw sets off in the morning, leaving Joseph, his trusty servant, to superintend the business of the farm. He returns, three days later, at eleven o'clock at night. He is 'fatigued'. I once walked 120 miles non-stop.* It is, indeed, 'fatiguing'. Mr Earnshaw is not a young man nor, we may suspect, hale. He dies six years later.

Hindley's fiddle is broken; the whip is, apparently, lost somewhere. But Earnshaw has brought a six-year-old child,

---

* See *The Boy Who Loved Books*, pp. 202–7. It was in the army and, in hospital for two weeks thereafter, I was threatened with being charged for damaging army property. Myself. My legs still twinge a bit reading this episode in *Wuthering Heights*.

dark-skinned, who speaks no English – just 'gibberish'. Carrying him would have made a 60-mile walk that much more burdensome.

Mrs Earnshaw promptly demands the 'gipsy brat' be thrown out. But her husband, now and later, is fond of the waif. Another oddness. He explains the child was starving, homeless, alone and that no 'owner' (not 'parent'; Liverpool is a slave trading port) could be found.

If Earnshaw has been away three days, a 60-mile bash in either direction (at a gruelling three miles an hour, across rough country and hills) would mean two 20-hour stints – assuming he did not stop to eat or sleep. Can one believe he wouldn't have to? Emily was the great walker in the family and would, presumably, have worked all this out.

So the questions are these: (1) Why go to far-off Liverpool, for a day visit, without any stated reason, at the least convenient time of year?; (2) Why walk, not ride?; (3) What could Earnshaw possibly achieve, in an advanced state of fatigue, in the few hours intervening between his epic walks to and fro?

Mrs Earnshaw's rage is a telling detail. She perhaps suspects that Mr Earnshaw has not been to Liverpool at all, but to some nearby gipsy encampments. Gipsies were famous for offering sexual services – brothels in caravans. Tolstoy was forever spending wild nights with gipsies, and infecting himself with unmentionable diseases in the process. The most famous burlesque artiste in history, Gipsy Rose Lee, embodies the allure of Romany. A fiddle would easily be picked up: gipsies were musical. And they had their own language, incomprehensible to English folk.

I lean, moderately, towards this speculative answer to the above questions. But I lean more heavily towards another, equally speculative. The 1770s were a boom period for the slave trade in Liverpool. Two vessels, with their forlorn cargo, would dock every week, traversing the golden triangle (Africa to England, to the West Indies; back, with sugar, to England, and Africa).

Mr Earnshaw is short-handed at Wuthering Heights; so much we may deduce. He needs hands. Apprentice hands if necessary. He already has doubts about Hindley. He will acquire, or buy, someone. Heathcliff comes attractively cheap. And he's not coal black, although, dark as he is, may be mixed race.

There are other genealogies. The Irish Marxist, Terry Eagleton, argues that Heathcliff has been dumped in the Liverpool streets by Irish migrants, fleeing the Great Hunger. The boy speaks Gaelic. There were millions fleeing Ireland in the mid-1840s, famine years, when *Wuthering Heights* was being written. But Heathcliff's arrival is dated 70 years earlier.

The suggestion that Heathcliff is Earnshaw's bastard child is rather less improbable than that he is demon spawn, dropped on the cursed house, by a wicked, fairy, stepmother. Or that the previous Heathcliff (see 'Mononymity', page 92) was beaten to death, and this later Heathcliff is his supernatural revenge. Speculation about Mr Earnshaw's walk, one can be sure, will continue to rage.

MASCULINITIES

There is a feminist lobby which claims Emily Brontë as a rebel against rigidly binary Victorian sexuality – a free, self-identifying woman before her time. The claim is helped by the near-total absence of hard detail around Emily's life. Nature may hate a vacuum: literary biography loves them.

A full-blooded assertion of the thesis is *Emily Brontë: Heretic* (1997), a novel by Stevie Davies, under the imprint of the Women's Press. It is, Davies says, her 'intuition' that Emily was a lesbian (though not enabled, by the times, to be a practising one). Intuitions are, arguably, as much an act of faith as crediting Emily 'channelling' *Wuthering Heights II* from beyond the veil (see below, 'Spirit-Written', page 144).

The first book to argue the lesbian case at length was Virginia Moore's passionate *The Life and Eager Death of Emily Brontë* (1936). 'Eager' because Emily lived in a world which denied her any opportunity to be herself. Self-mortification and, ultimately, self-destruction was the only way out. That and silence.

As regards evidence which, as lawyers say, 'stands up' we have only straws to clutch at. The sisters' use of male pseudonyms could have been something more than tactical. 'Ellis Bell' would, they claimed to believe, get more attention in the man's world of publishing than, say, 'Alice Bell'. George Eliot thought the same. True enough. But perhaps the sisters, Emily particularly, liked the idea of male masquerade. It was a kind of authorial Bloomerism.* Trying on the trousers that ruled.

Women shared (small) beds in the 19th century, for the good reason that there was no space for separate rooms. For women it was a sardine-tin world. Their bodies, in flimsy night-dresses, touched. Bodily warmth entailed intimate contact. Emily held a school teaching position at Law Hill, Halifax (September

---

* The American Amelia Jenks Bloomer (1818–1894) pioneered, among other feminist reforms, 'rational dress' – trousers, principally – for women. 'Bloomerism' was much ridiculed in the 1850s and after, although, as a cursory look round any street will verify, Ms Bloomer had the last laugh.

1838–March 1839; the boarding school building, and its history, may have contributed something to *Wuthering Heights* – not least its high hillside position which 'wuthered' noisily). Perhaps, it's speculated, the late-teenaged, post-pubescent, Emily formed briefly intimate relationships. There's a lot of 'perhaps' on this topic.

Charlotte judged Emily to be 'stronger than a man'. The two sisters' professor in Belgium, M. Héger, went so far as to assert Emily 'should have been a man'. She was nicknamed 'Major' in the family. The publisher George Smith (who took over the copyright of *Wuthering Heights* after her death) detected in Emily a 'singularly masculine bent of intellect'. Singularly? Masculine? Haworth villagers are reported of thinking her 'more like a boy than a girl'. Ellen Nussey noted that she whistled to her dogs in 'masculine fashion'. Her taste in four-legged companions (see above, 'The Hound of Haworth', page 62) was distinctly other than a ladies' lap-dog.

Charlotte tells us that Shirley Keeldar is a portrait of her sister. The heroine was called 'Shirley' (a male/female name) because her parents had, for years before her belated birth, wanted a son. Shirley plays the part, assuming male privilege in her business affairs, as an 'of-age' heir(ess):

> Business! Really the word makes me conscious I am indeed no longer a girl, but quite a woman and something more. I am an esquire! Shirley Keeldar, Esquire, ought to be my style and title. They gave me a man's name; I hold a man's position. It is enough to inspire me with a touch of manhood; and when I see such people as that stately Anglo-Belgian – that Gérard Moore – before me, gravely talking to me of business, really I feel quite

gentlemanlike. You must choose me for your church-
warden, Mr. Helstone, the next time you elect new ones.
They ought to make me a magistrate and a captain of
yeomanry. Tony Lumpkin's mother was a colonel, and his
aunt a justice of the peace. Why shouldn't I be?

If this masculinised portrait is a covert hint, it would fit into the
dominant 19th-century theory that homosexuality was 'inverted'
sexuality. Unlucky men discovered themselves, by the perverse
throw of the genetic dice, trapped inside a female body, and vice
versa. Sexual inversion was theorised 'scientifically' by the psy-
chologist Havelock Ellis and romanticised for a later generation
by 'John' Radclyffe Hall's novel *The Well of Loneliness* and its
hero/heroine 'Stephen'. It's no longer regarded as valid sexology.
Nonetheless, Catherine's exclamation, 'I am Heathcliff', and the
strange asexuality of their relationship has been built on to make
the case that *Wuthering Heights* is, for the informed reader, 'a
lesbian text'.

A thoughtful argument on the subject is advanced by Jean E.
Kennard.* Kennard opens with the question 'What did Charlotte
destroy?' Answers are ventured. After Emily's death, Charlotte
was her sister's (unofficial) executor. Charlotte's care of Emily's
literary remains was anything but curatorial. It seems 'probable',
says Kennard,

that Charlotte destroyed her sister's posthumous papers.
She published only 17 of the 103 poems extant after
death, and those she reworked. There are no remaining

* 'Lesbianism and the Censoring of *Wuthering Heights*', *NWSA Journal*,
(Summer, 1996).

letters between Emily and her family, no prose juvenilia, and very few diary entries, although we know that
Emily wrote frequently to her sister Anne when they
were apart and kept a diary. Charlotte herself acknow-
ledged that manuscripts of her sister's writings existed
after her death.

Kennard goes on to speculate whether Charlotte 'censored'
material 'too personal to publish'. She cleaned up the family
mess. The Brontë image should be forever unsullied. The truth
is, we shall never know. If Emily Brontë's life was devoted to anything, it was devoted to creating a *noli me tangere* around herself.
Charlotte's destruction of materials may have been, it would be
nice to think, a last act of loving respect for her sister's lifelong
wish. 'Let me alone.' Do not touch me.

MONONYMITY

Readers often query Heathcliff's lack of any Christian name.
There is an obvious reason: he's not a Christian. He belongs to
another. As Joseph says, by way of obituary, 'Th' divil's harried
off his soul.'*

There is no suggestion, when the mewling six-year-old is
brought to Wuthering Heights, that he is religiously baptised.

---

* Joseph says 'harried', not 'carried' because—primitive theologian
that he is—he's thinking of the harrowing of hell: that visit by Christ,
between Crucifixion and Resurrection, to the underworld to work out
which are his, and which are Satan's.

The Holy Water would (as in *The Omen*) have sizzled like acid on the foundling's brow. Catherine spits on him by way of blessing.

He is given the name of a previous child who died in childhood. It was, in the 18th century, a common practice. Walter Scott (born at the same period as Heathcliff) was given the same Christian name as a pre-deceased sibling. Infant mortality ran so high (only five out of nine of Walter's siblings survived) that it was a kind of living memorial to those who came and went before they were even known.

We know nothing about Heathcliff (the first) other than his name and the fact he left the world young. His full name, of course, would have been Heathcliff Earnshaw and his little body is, doubtless, interred where his mother, sister Catherine, and namesake (less half the name) are later buried. Gimmerton Kirk.

The name, 'Heathcliff', is not one routinely found in the baptism registers of the English Church. But it brings with it a windy blast of the moors – as does Hindley (a name since made forever sinister by the 'Moors Murderer', Myra Hindley). In the 18th century the Hindley area, round Manchester, was moorish. Earnshaw, etymologically, means 'eagle shelter'. Emily gave such things thought.

Heathcliff (the second), of course, is not of the family blood and cannot have its surname unless adopted. But everyone is happy, apparently, that Heathcliff should serves him as forename and surname.

What is done, and not done with names always merits consideration in the Brontës' fiction. Shirley (a male and female name in the 19th century) had no second Christian name because, we are told, her parents were longing for a son. The hardness of her character went only halfway to answering that desire.

Heathcliff's mononymity connects him with the animal world (Emily's 'Keeper', for example), and slavery. Does anyone know what Uncle Tom's surname is, or Jim's, in *Huckleberry Finn?* They have none. There is a strong line of speculation that Heathcliff is the offspring of a slave parent – male or female – and is mixed race.

The question of Heathcliff's single name bubbles up in the magnificent final sentences of *Wuthering Heights*. Gimmerton Kirk has fallen into decay (Methodism has made terrible inroads). It has no minister, and is, presumably, deconsecrated. The moor (heath and cliff) is repossessing the graveyard. Lockwood describes it on a warm summer evening, not a 'wuther' to be felt:

> My walk home was lengthened by a diversion in the direction of the kirk. When beneath its walls, I perceived decay had made progress, even in seven months: many a window showed black gaps deprived of glass; and slates jutted off here and there, beyond the right line of the roof, to be gradually worked off in coming autumn storms.
>
> I sought, and soon discovered, the three headstones on the slope next the moor: the middle one grey, and half buried in the heath; Edgar Linton's only harmonised by the turf and moss creeping up its foot; Heathcliff's still bare.

Nameless in death, as he was in birth. No service has been read over his coffin; there is no inscription on his stone. He goes as he came.

MR CHARLOTTE BRONTË

We don't call her 'Mrs Nicholls'; nor would she want us to. She left such marital obeisance to 'Mrs Gaskell' and 'Mrs Humphry Ward', two of her greatest posthumous champions.

Arthur Bell Nicholls (1819–1906) was a curate – assistant to the perpetual Haworth curate, Patrick Brontë, from May 1845 until 1861. Nicholls was Northern Irish Anglican. He was Trinity College Dublin-educated and less intellectual than the Cambridge-educated Patrick.

The epithet applied to Arthur behind his back was 'ox-like' – appropriately Homeric. He was recruited as a clerical beast of burden. Patrick was, in his career, severely afflicted with eye problems. But he was unable to retire given his measly pension, stipendiary prospects and the desperate necessity of retaining the only roof over his head (a rather fine one, as it happened) that was available to him. He stumbled blindly on.

There is speculation that the new curate may have inspired Acton, Ellis and Currer's pen-surname, which they adopted into their 'Bell' scheme around the time of his arrival at Haworth. But not much can be made of that idea. Except that Arthur Bell Nicholls may have been a figure of fun rather than any romantic interest for the daughters of the house.

The sisters were not overwhelmed with the big, bull-headed Irishman in his early days at Haworth: they were not overly keen on anything from that nation (he may, plausibly, have inspired something of the vulgar Irish curate Malone in *Shirley*, but very little of the saintly and theologically clever English curate Weston in *Agnes Grey*). Charlotte put down very sharply, soon after he arrived, the gossip that she was going to marry the Revd Bell. The loose talk was, in the event, prophetic.

Charlotte, in her thoughts about the man who should be her partner, aspired higher. But Constantin Héger was impossible and George Smith, her publisher, upon whom she also had designs, liked her, but was not in love with her. Alone in the world, all her five siblings gone, with a disabled father to support, she was disposed to find a humbler companion to help her care for Patrick.

Even so, the route to the altar with the woman he aspired to love was not easy for Arthur. His first proposal was made with 'trepidation'. He shook 'head to toe' with apprehension while declaring his love to Charlotte. He was right to be nervous. His putative father-in-law was apoplectic at his curate's presumption.

Patrick was aged, virtually blind, and increasingly dependent on his one surviving child (she, too, was approaching middle-age, and frail). Charlotte's income, as one of the country's most renowned authors, was also necessary to the two surviving Brontës. His age and infirmity would be wretched without the comforts her bestselling books now provided. The fact was that he did not, as Charlotte confided to Ellen Nussey, want his last daughter to marry *anyone*. It would be like kicking the blind man's dog (Nicholls was kind to dogs, particularly Flossy, now fat and aged herself – one of the things eventually found in his favour).

When he realised how fiercely Patrick opposed the marriage (the veins on his head had stood out like whipcord, and his eyes went bloodshot when he learned of the proposal, Charlotte reported), Nicholls melodramatically applied to take the Christian message to Australia. Let Nicholls go there to convert the transported criminals and God-forsaken aboriginals, Patrick said. There wasn't enough gold ore in the outback diggings, he

The Revd Patrick Brontë late in life. His wife and most of his children are dead, his eyes are failing. He suffers, stoically.

declared, (it was the period of the gold rush) to qualify Nicholls as husband for his Charlotte.

Initially Charlotte turned the importunate curate down. By letter. But Arthur went on to play his cards astutely: he went on a fast unto death. He made it clear that his starvation should be known. He melodramatically collapsed while giving his sermon, in a welter of tears, in front of the bewildered Haworth congregation, who may have thought he had gone Pentecostalist and would start babbling to them in tongues.

The Revd Nicholls was not by nature an emotional preacher, or indeed an emotional anything. 'Unmanly drivelling', Patrick's party proclaimed it. But Arthur's strategy was shrewd. He applied not for Charlotte's love (he would never get that) but her pity. She was flattered by his ostentatious woe and genuinely sympathetic. He would die, or go to the ends of the earth, for her. If he remained in Haworth (crippling 'rheumatic pains' had come on, getting in the way of the Antipodean scheme) he would die of inanition. It was reported to the parsonage, by the servant telegraphy, that the Revd Arthur pushed away his plate and would eat nothing.

Charlotte kept her woebegone suitor in play for months. Her remarks in letters to friends about him were less than warm. Mrs Gaskell, one adviser, was of the Nicholls party, and pushed the curate's suit. Ellen Nussey was not a supporter. She, like Patrick, was against any marriage at all for Charlotte, at her age (late thirties) and in her physical condition.

No move was made. It was not entirely indecision. All this while Charlotte had another string to her bow. Her hopes were secretly directed at George Smith, the 'Prince of Publishers' (as the book trade called him), who had saved her from the fates of Emily and Anne at the hands of the rogue T.C. Newby (see below, 'Publishers', page 137).

George Smith it was who had commissioned the glamorising Richmond portrait (see page 155). Was that not the act of a lover? He also gave Charlotte the other picture which occupied a place of honour alongside hers in the Haworth parlour. It was of Smith's other top-billed author, and Charlotte's idol, Thackeray. Was that not the act of a staunch admirer? He underpaid her, granted – the fate of most women writers.* But he was a judicious adviser, on literary matters, on money (buy annuities, he instructed, not shares) and on how to act as the executor of the Brontë literary estate. Was that not the act of someone with a long-term interest in her?

Charlotte was in the habit of sending her love-letters in the form of fiction. There are two such in *Villette*. One is to M. Héger, in the fictional person of Paul Emanuel. The other is to George Smith, in the fictional person of 'Dr John'.

Bluntly, Charlotte fooled herself into thinking George Smith might marry her. She evaded Nicholls' increasingly embarrassing foolery by taking refuge in Smith's London household. It cannot have been entirely comfortable. George's mother had never liked Miss Brontë much, nor the depiction of her son as 'Dr John'. Least of all had she liked the depiction of herself as 'Mrs Bretton'. But she was hospitable to the Yorkshire refugee. The old lady would come round, Charlotte must have believed.

Marriage with George Smith would, from the Haworth point of view, have been a perfect match. He was rich, and a man of the world. Thackeray had thought him, initially, somewhat sullied by 'trade' (Smith, Elder's wealth came substantially from Apollinaris mineral water). George had begun as an apprentice in the family firm. A working-man. Thackeray helped frame him into something more gentlemanlike (getting him into the Reform Club, for example).

* Smith paid Charlotte half what he paid his male stars, e.g. £500 for *Villette* as against, at the same period, £1,000 for Thackeray's *Esmond*.

'Prince of publishers' George Smith

Smith, a superb reader of text, quite well knew what
Charlotte was getting at in *Villette*, vis-à-vis himself. But he could
never love her: she was not 'pretty', she was not young (seven
years older than him). And there were those (missing) teeth.
His snappers, as described in *Villette*, along with his glorious
aureole of hair, were perfect. Years later, he confided his feelings
about Charlotte, with rather distasteful candour, to another of
his protégées, Mrs Humphry Ward, author of *Robert Elsmere*,
whose career he tended as solicitously, and imaginatively, as he
had tended that of the author of *Jane Eyre*:

No, I never was in the least bit in love with Charlotte
Brontë … I never could have loved any woman who had
not some charm or grace of person, and Charlotte Brontë
had none – I liked her and was interested in her, and I
admired her – especially when she was in Yorkshire and
I was in London. I never was coxcomb enough to suppose that she was in love with me. But I believe that my
mother was at one time rather alarmed.

In the letters she wrote over these precarious weeks Charlotte
observes to her friends how prematurely 'aged' Smith looked.
She evidently hoped that fact (which may have been imaginary)
compensated for the seven-year gulf in age.

Her hopes came to nothing when, out of the blue, Smith
became engaged to young and attractive (and unliterary)
Elizabeth Blakeway. His mother passed on the news. Charlotte
was hurt and furious. She wrote an offensively frigid letter of
congratulation, returned unopened the parcels of books Smith
regularly sent her, and informed him her books would henceforth
go elsewhere. She acted, in short, like a woman scorned. Smith
was no longer the Prince of Publishers but a trifler.

She returned to Haworth and Nicholls, still martyring himself for love. His star was in the ascendant. There was no more
talk of Australia. But arrangements needed to be made. Charlotte
ensured that the annuities Smith had advised her to invest in
would remain hers for the benefit of her father, if she died first.
She did not want her money, should she predecease her husband, draining away to unknown in-laws in Ireland. Realistically,
a life insurance salesman would estimate that he had the better
prospects of long life. Although seven years older than Charlotte,
Arthur was of sturdy peasant stock and would, it transpired,

outlive his chronically sick wife by half a century. Residence after marriage, Arthur was instructed, would continue to be at Haworth, the better to care for Patrick: she domestically, he in church matters. It meant perpetual subordination for Charlotte's spouse. There should be no publicity about 'Currer Bell' getting married.

Arthur deferred, humbly, to all these requirements. 'Mr Nicholls is a kind, considerate fellow,' Charlotte wrote, 'with all his masculine faults, he enters into my wishes about having the thing done quietly.' The 'thing'? And what, precisely, were his 'masculine faults'? But his premarital submission was promising: 'I trust the demands of both feeling and duty,' she wrote, 'will be in some measure reconciled by the step in contemplation.' It's a chillingly businesslike tone.

The couple took the 'step in contemplation' on 29 June 1854. Patrick did not officiate or attend. It was a tiny ceremony. All Charlotte's sisters had gone to their graves young virgins. She, now a middle-aged woman of 37, was the only daughter to experience sexual intercourse. It killed her. Along with her unborn child, she died eight months after marriage – possibly, as has been argued, from severe morning sickness.

Arthur remained at Haworth, looking after his father-in-law. When Patrick died, in June 1861, his subordinate expected to take over as perpetual curate. He deserved to, but the vote of the local committee went against him. Congregations had, over the years, always found him rather 'stiff'. He retired to Ireland, remarried (childlessly) and was, if not cheated, eased out of what control he had over Charlotte's literary legacy and literary remains. He gave up the cloth and died in 1906. What he knew about the Brontës – more than any critic or biographer has – he took to the grave.

A fine photograph of the Revd Arthur Bell Nicholls in later
life but reflecting something of the power of his personality.
It was 'will' which won Charlotte as his wife.

MRS ARTHUR BELL NICHOLLS

Charlotte's taking her business from George Smith (because
he married another woman) was pettish, small-minded, and
ill-advised.

Arthur was, all evidence suggests, a thoroughly decent and
humble man. At least when it came to literature. Charlotte could
have done worse. He had been her slave before marriage. But
with the rings on their fingers he came into conjugal rights, and
exercised them. By law and the sterner dictates of the holy writ
he lived by, Arthur Bell Nicholls was now lord and master.

The couple's honeymoon was passed in Ireland, where his family was introduced. Unlike Patrick, he was not going to disown those he came from; nor should his wife cut them out. He began censoring her letters to friends who had known her for years. He demanded to read them before they were sent and came close to prohibiting any communication at all with correspondents like Ellen Nussey, who he knew disapproved of the marriage and him (after Charlotte's death she would maintain Arthur was a killer).

Charlotte's letters reveal her discovery that he had long disapproved of the lack of ecclesiastical stringency in her writing. The curates' scene at the opening of *Shirley*, for example, and the cutting satire against the Irish Malone in that novel. He specifically criticised the 'latitudinarian' sneers against the stern simplicities of evangelical baptism, and, implicitly, her suggestive sympathy for Rome. The passage which particularly rankled could be read as something aimed directly at him, or curates like him. In the opening paragraphs of *Shirley* Charlotte wrote:

> Curates were scarce then: there was no Pastoral Aid – no Additional Curates' Society to stretch a helping hand to worn-out old rectors and incumbents, and give them the wherewithal to pay a vigorous young colleague from Oxford or Cambridge. The present successors of the apostles, disciples of Dr. Pusey and tools of the Propaganda, were at that time being hatched under cradle-blankets, or undergoing regeneration by nursery-baptism in wash-hand basins.

There should be, Arthur may have thought, no more of that nonsense in his spouse's fiction.

Devoted as he was to her, had she lived, without George Smith behind her, Charlotte Brontë would, one suspects, have been a novelist in marital shackles. Would Charlotte have kissed the rod (she was obedient in the first months of marriage) or, eventually, have exploded into rebellion?

MURDER?

Is Edward Rochester a murderer?

The only book of litcrit I have written which has ever found its way to a bestseller list was *Is Heathcliff a Murderer?* Glorious week.

The case against the brute of Wuthering Heights is open and shut from circumstantial evidence. No Sherlock needed. To my mind Heathcliff unquestionably killed Hindley, having sent the other resident in the house, Joseph, off to Dr Ken. He (probably) helped his drunken victim into the next world with a pillow over his face. If there was any justice on the Gimmerton Assize Circuit, Heathcliff ought to have swung before he could create more havoc in the West Riding.

That Rochester is a would-be bigamist is similarly clear-cut. The evidence as to uxoricide is, admittedly, less overwhelming than it is with Heathcliff's homicide, but a powerful prosecution case can be made that the convenient disposal of Mrs Edward Rochester (universally derogated as 'Bertha Mason') is murder.

Although Rochester claims 'indirect assassination is not in his nature', this would seem to be exactly how he clears the first Mrs Rochester out of the way, acquiring willing Jane to fill the vacant role. He may have kept the poor deranged woman at deserted Thornfield Hall for just that nefarious purpose. It was, with the right connections, possible to get a divorce by Act of

Parliament but it was impossible to divorce a wife who was not *compos mentis*. Thackeray, aching as he was for another wife, could not divorce his luckless, schizophrenic, Isabella.

The description of Bertha's death is given to Jane in the Rochester Arms, as she is on the last leg of her obeying Rochester's ethereal summons (see above, 'Jane! Jane! Jane!', page 71). The public house is not, one would guess, a place where Edward Rochester would be spoken ill of by anyone wanting to carrying on pulling pints behind the bar.

The innkeeper recounts the event, as Jane, ignorant even about the fire which has destroyed Thornfield, takes her breakfast:

> 'Yes, indeed was he; and he went up to the attics when all was burning above and below, and got the servants out of their beds and helped them down himself, and went back to get his mad wife out of her cell. And then they called out to him that she was on the roof, where she was standing, waving her arms, above the battlements, and shouting out till they could hear her a mile off: I saw her and heard her with my own eyes. She was a big woman, and had long black hair: we could see it streaming against the flames as she stood. I witnessed, and several more witnessed, Mr. Rochester ascend through the skylight on to the roof; we heard him call "Bertha!" We saw him approach her; and then, ma'am, she yelled and gave a spring, and the next minute she lay smashed on the pavement.'

> 'Dead?'

> 'Dead! Ay, dead as the stones on which her brains and blood were scattered.'

Jane's fork, one fancifully visualises, must have paused over her breakfast black pudding. It is clear from the form of words ('I *witnessed* and several more *witnessed*') that the innkeeper, formerly the Thornfield butler, is parroting verbatim his (and fellow servants') rigidly dutiful testimony at the coroner's inquest. As a lifelong pensioner of the Rochesters, he would have been a fool not to have said in the witness stand what his paymaster required him to say. Damn the oath.

There is no clear evidence that Edward went up to the burning roof to *save* Bertha. And at the very least Mr Rochester, if no wife-murderer, might be thought indictable for manslaughter by virtue of persistent and longstanding neglect. Mrs Poole should surely have been let go to get negligently drunk elsewhere (or did she know too much about what was going on at Thornfield to be dismissed?)

The jury will be forever out on Rochester, but my verdict is guilty. My belief? He killed the woman.

MYOPIA

Visitors to the Brontë Museum (having braved the Brontë tat-fest and theme park which is now Haworth) will probably look with passing curiosity at Charlotte Brontë's 'specs'. They are folding tortoiseshell lorgnettes – the kind of spectacles which are most easily put on, and taken off.

Charlotte did not, one gathers, like being seen with her visual aids on but was bat-blind without them. The Haworth lenses are measured at minus 10 dioptres, which grades as 'severe short sight'. Stumblingly myopic.

None of the surviving pictures of the sisters show any of

them with glasses, although there was short-sightedness through-out the family. Branwell, images attest, did not mind being bespectacled.

Mrs Gaskell notes the weakness of Charlotte's eyes and offers an explanation:

> She cannot see well, and does little beside knitting. The way she weakened her eyesight was this: When she was sixteen or seventeen, she wanted much to draw; and she copied nimini-pimini copper-plate engravings out of annuals, ('stippling,' don't the artists call it?) every little point put in, till at the end of six months she had pro-duced an exquisitely faithful copy of the engraving. She wanted to learn to express her ideas by drawing. After she had tried to draw stories, and not succeeded, she took the better mode of writing; but in so small a hand, that it is almost impossible to decipher what she wrote at this time.

In fact, as Juliet Barker notes, there is evidence that Charlotte's short-sightedness was not the result of eye-strain in adoles-cence, but inherited. Charlotte could not join in sports at school, because she could not see beyond her nose. More consequentially, she could not learn a musical instrument because she had to lean so close to the score that her hands had no room to move across the keys.

Gaskell is right, however, about the short-sightedness acting as a kind of protective screen for her writing. At the time the sis-ters were composing their mature works, their father was virtually blind with cataracts (the operation to cure them, with scalpel and without anaesthetic, a terrifying thought). Branwell was, in the years leading to his death, blind drunk. He did, however, in earlier years, collaborate on the notebooks which contain the Gondal/ Angria sagas. The privacy of these creations was preserved by the smallness of the script. The lettering is so small as to be encoded.

The 'Professor', William Crimsworth, notes, parenthetically, that he is short-sighted (although Edmund Dulac's illustrations in the 1905 edition – see above, 'The Idiot Child and Me', page 69 – do not show him with spectacles). Spectacles are, however, central props in *Villette*. The first eruption of Paul Emanuel (the professor/master) into Lucy Snowe's life focuses on them:

> The teacher ran to the salon door. M. Paul was summoned. He entered: a small, dark and spare man, in spectacles.
>
> 'Mon cousin,' began Madame, 'I want your opinion. We know your skill in physiognomy; use it now. Read that countenance.'
>
> The little man fixed on me his spectacles: A resolute compression of the lips, and gathering of the brow, seemed to say that he meant to see through me, and that a veil would be no veil for him.

'Thou God Seest Me', as the favourite Victorian inscription has it. Emanuel uses light steel-framed 'lunettes', worn all day long.

In the crisis of the story, Lucy breaks the sacred lunettes. It is an accident, but he 'vociferates' thunderingly in his rage at being deprived of his vision:

> 'Là!' said he: 'me voilà veuf [widowed] de mes lunettes! I think Mademoiselle Lucy will now confess that the cord and gallows are amply earned; she trembles in

anticipation of her doom. Ah, traitress! traitress! You are resolved to have me quite blind and helpless in your hands!'

Emanuel Agonistes. One recalls the Samsonically blind Rochester. Lucy is the man-destroying Delilah.

It may strike the modern reader as quaint. All this ado over – what? – a pair of specs? But the symbolism resonates.

There is a larger issue. The three sisters had one glorious ambition in their adult life: to set up a school. Schoolteaching was one of the very few 'professions' available to women of mental ability. And one of the features of the school environment was that spectacles were not disfiguring but, as with Emanuel, indices of teacherly distinction – along with the gown (and cane). In the schoolroom, Charlotte could have worn her glasses with pride.

NO COWARD SOUL

The Brontës' poetry has been respected, but never admired as much as has the prose fiction. Their spectacular veer into the writing of three-volume novels might, of course, have been forestalled had the major poets of the age whom they consulted – Southey, Coleridge and Wordsworth – been more encouraging. They singularly weren't encouraging.

There is one exception, Emily's 'No Coward Soul Is Mine', known universally by its fighting first line, has been applauded as one of the greatest religious poems of the century.

The seven-stanza lyric was published, under Charlotte's authorisation, in an 1850 volume, with the comment 'the following are the last lines my sister Emily ever wrote'. She had been dead two years. The detail added a dark lustre to the poem. It joins a select group, along with Donne's 'Hymne to God, my God in my Sicknesse' (supposedly written on his deathbed) and, more recently, David Bowie's 'Lazarus' (not, perhaps, company Emily would have wanted to keep).

Charlotte's dating was taken as gospel. Emily Dickinson, who felt a strong kinship with the Yorkshire Emily, requested, on her deathbed, that the poem be read out by a trusted friend at her funeral.

In point of fact recent scholarship has established that Charlotte's dating was amiss. The poem was composed in early January 1846, around the time Charlotte's 'invasion' of Emily's private papers, to put together the contents of the *Poems* volume, provoked an awful row between the sisters. There is, apparently, an even earlier proto-version of 'No Coward Soul' in the juvenile Gondal manuscripts. Charlotte, who was in charge of the ill-fated Bell poems, must surely have known the true chronology and yet publicised (the 'last lines' detail is radioactive) a false one.

Her reasons for (1) not publishing 'No Coward Soul' in the printed volume and (2) giving it a false origin can only be speculated on. I speculate it was the assertive egocentric theology of the poem which offended the more religiously orthodox Charlotte: Emily's frank boast that God was within her, that she was pregnant with divinity, and that God would still be there, were the whole universe (stars, planets and all) destroyed. It implies a singularly personal relationship with the Almighty. A dying woman, *in articulo mortis*, might get away with it. Just.

Charlotte's wilful misrepresentation of 'No Coward Soul' is just one example of a generally proprietary practice with her sisters' work, verging at times on the high-handed. There are others. George Smith wanted to rescue Emily and Anne's first novels from the rogue Newby (see below, 'Publishers', page 137). The sisters reportedly declined. I can't believe Charlotte could not have persuaded them to transfer. But, under the 'Bell' nom de plume, the sibling relationship would have been made much of by a press which was already giving the novels a hammering.

The following is the published text of 'No Coward Soul Is Mine':

> No coward soul is mine,
> No trembler in the world's storm-troubled sphere:
> I see Heaven's glories shine,
> And faith shines equal arming me from fear.
>
> O God within my breast,
> Almighty ever-present Deity!
> Life—that in me hast rest,
> As I—Undying Life—have power in Thee!
>
> Vain are the thousand creeds
> That move men's hearts: unutterably vain;
> Worthless as withered weeds,
> Or idlest froth amid the boundless main,
>
> To waken doubt in one
> Holding so fast by Thine infinity;
> So surely anchored on
> The steadfast rock of immortality.
>
> With wide-embracing love
> Thy spirit animates eternal years,
> Pervades and broods above,
> Changes, sustains, dissolves, creates and rears

Though Earth and moon were gone,
And suns and universes ceased to be,
And Thou wert left alone,
Every Existence would exist in Thee.

There is not room for Death,
Nor atom that his might could render void:
Thou—Thou art Being and Breath,
And what Thou art may never be destroyed.

The poem ranks as the most moving Charlotte ever allowed into publication.

NORMALITY?

On 22 October 2015, the *Daily Mail* ran a story under the screaming headline:

The brutal Brontës! Emily beat up her pet dog. Charlotte – plain, toothless and dull – was so spiteful children threw stones at her!

The article was over an edited extract of Claire Harman's (entirely balanced) biography, *Charlotte Brontë: A Life*.

Ah yes, one mutters, the 'brutal' Brontës. But why stop there. Haworth was – what did Daphne du Maurier call it? – an 'inferno'. Montage pictures come to mind: opium-maddened Branwell attempting to burn his father to death in his bed (a scene immortalised soon after in *Jane Eyre*). Patrick himself is meanwhile firing his pistol like a drink-maddened cowpuncher on

Saturday night in Dodge City. A wild colonial boy in a dog-collar. The strangely remote children drift aerially like ghosts, indifferent to any world outside their own, trapped in their self-woven 'web of childhood'. There must be children in the attic – and in another attic the first Mrs Brontë, ranting madly. Outside, the wind 'wuthers' (who else uses that word?) against the parsonage over the thorns, cockles and tares of wildest Yorkshire. Emily? A room of her own? Pah! Hers was a more rugged feminism. All that fiery spirit needed was a *moor* of her own. Rabid dogs wander the streets of the town. Heat a poker white-hot to cauterise the bite wounds and beat your own hound blind if he dares lie on your bed. TB ravages those who survived Yorkshire schools which made Wackford Squeers's academy look like Cheltenham Ladies' College on parents' day.

Juliet Barker wrote her massive, deeply researched biography in 1994, with the declared aim of sweeping the cloud of Brontëan mythopoeia, such as the above, into the dustbin of literary biography. There is a bucket of cold water on every one of Barker's 800 or so pages. The Brontë children, she insists 'had a perfectly normal childhood'. For the time and place, of course.

They were, as Barker depicts, outgoing and fun-loving kids. Did not the whole of their writing careers begin with the gift of a dozen toy soldiers to Branwell? Patrick Brontë, as Barker revises his portrait, was a liberal, conscientious, hardworking, intellectually curious clergyman. And a good parent. A very interesting man all round, if one takes the trouble to look at him. Cowan Bridge was not a good school, but by current Yorkshire standards (as many graduates who read *Jane Eyre* enragedly testified) not *that* bad. Lowood was, pure and simple, exaggeration.

The mythic Brontëmania originates with Mrs Gaskell, and the poison fruit of the tree (notably the venomous testimony of the dismissed servant, Martha Wright) she gave too ready a credence to. Every reader interested in the Brontës should read Barker's corrective work, whose dullness is strategic. It serves as biographical coolant.

But, somehow the Brontë myth-mania will not die. The flames leap back despite Barker's dousing. Ten years after her book was published, for example, under the emetic headline: 'Reader, I Shagged him: Why Charlotte Brontë was a Filthy Minx', the *Guardian* (25 March 2005) ran an article which asserted, in its subtitle:

> Since her death 150 years ago, Charlotte Brontë has been sanitised as a dull, Gothic drudge. Far from it, says Tanya Gold; the author was a filthy, frustrated, sex-obsessed genius.

The compliment 'genius' rather wilts in the glare of Charlotte's proclaimed dedication to 'shagging'. One visualises her emerging guiltily from behind some convenient bush in Haworth moorland, rearranging her skirts.

To dip in one's thumb and pluck out the kind of plum one would rather not eat, consider the following from Ms Gold:

> As the 150th anniversary of her death on 31 March 1855 approaches, it is time to rescue Charlotte Brontë. She has been chained, weeping, to a radiator in the Haworth Parsonage, Yorkshire, for too long. Enough of Gaskell's fake miserabilia. Enough of the Brontë industry's veneration of coffins, bonnets and tuberculosis. It is time to exhume the real Charlotte – filthy bitch, grandmother of chick-lit, and friend.

There is no evidence offered for this sensational depiction beyond what other commentators have read in a less inflammatory way. 'Normal' (even if true, which I believe it is) has a hard time triumphing with the Brontës. We love the myths too much. And, of course, they sell books, films, TV serials and tea cosies.

OBSTINATE FASTING

The sisters would have looked blankly at the term 'anorexia nervosa'. But they knew what it was, in the flesh, better than most. They were themselves 'hunger artists'. And, when needed, pioneers of the pre-Ghandian political fast unto death.

When their beloved Tabitha Aykroyd (a 'stout' woman who outlived them all), mistress of the kitchen, faced dismissal the sisters went on hunger strike to keep her. Emily, by refusing food, got herself sent home from her school, Roe Head. Yorkshire schools always had enough starved pupils to be getting on with.

Self-denial – even to the verge of self-destruction and beyond – was one of the readiest weapons the sisters had, domestically. There are few scenes of enjoyable eating in the sisters' fiction. One's saliva glands are untroubled. In Charlotte's fiction, the act of ingestion is, as described in the gluttony of the curates in *Shirley*, as ugly as the rumbling act of digestion and the wholly disgusting act of defecation.

And gluttony, like lechery, is what men do. Consider the following, from *Shirley*:

'You have your household in proper order,' observed Malone approvingly, as, with his fine face ruddy as the embers over which he bent, he assiduously turned the mutton chops. 'You are not under petticoat government, like poor Sweeting, a man – whew! how the fat spits! it has burnt my hand – destined to be ruled by women. Now you and I, Moore – there's a fine brown one for you, and full of gravy – you and I will have no grey mares in our stables when we marry.'

(The reference is to the proverb 'the grey mare is the better horse' – i.e. the woman rules the man.)

Starvation, total or partial, cut back on horrific trips to that awful three-seater bog at the back of the parsonage, queuing up behind servants or making way for the master of the house. My surmise is that Emily's long solitary walks on the moor were, at least partly, for matters of solitary relief.

Katherine Frank has written a book arguing that each of the three writing sisters would today 'almost certainly be diagnosed as suffering from Anorexia Nervosa'.* But of all of the sisters Emily used hunger most aggressively. She evidently gave it thought and refined those thoughts into what amounted to an idiosyncratic theology.

One suspects Emily was a devotee of Thomas à Kempis's *Imitation of Christ* and its grim instruction:

Jesus has many who love His Kingdom in Heaven, but few who bear His Cross (Luke 14:27). He has many who desire comfort, but few who desire suffering. He finds many to share His feast, but few His fasting.

* Katherine Frank, *A Chainless Soul: A Life of Emily Brontë* (1991).

Hunger was the royal road to spiritual purity. It was always Lenten fare with Emily Brontë.

The two principal characters in *Wuthering Heights*, the elder Cathy and Heathcliff, starve themselves to death. Their self-starving is stressed in two key scenes. The first is that between Ellen (a 'stout' woman) and Cathy. Her suicidal tendencies have already been put on record. Mr Kenneth (surely one of the least effective physicians in Victorian fiction) diagnoses her as dangerously self-harming: take care, he warns, 'that she not throw herself down stairs or out of the window'. Cathy would never do that. She wants a death which does not violate the purity of her body, or her corpse.

She embarks on her self-starvation with that peculiar egotism which all the principal characters in the novel exhibit. She is in the final weeks of pregnancy and, to borrow a phrase, not-eating for two. Little she cares if young Cathy is born brain-damaged.

Heathcliff chooses the same death by inanition. He denies himself all food and water, tormented as he is by the spectral image of malevolent Cathy outside the window, luring him to eternal togetherness beyond life. It takes three days for him to extinguish himself: not entirely plausible with a robust Yorkshire farmer. Again the stout Nelly, as she earlier did with Cathy, vainly attempts to talk sense into him.

Although she suffered from the occupational hazard of the Haworth household, there is no question that the proximate cause of Emily's death was self-starvation. As with Heathcliff, expiry was a rush job. She was always impatient, observed Charlotte, with a morbid jest – 'She made haste to leave us'.

Starvation takes – even with a frail bodily frame – weeks. Charlotte used the term 'wasted' twice: to describe Emily's aspect in her last days, and to describe her corpse, which she helped prepare for interment. In Charlotte's account there is a tinge of admiration – envy, almost – for the sheer purity of Emily's final act:

> Stronger than a man, simpler than a child, her nature stood alone. The awful point was that, while full of ruth for others, on herself she had no pity; the spirit was inexorable to the flesh; from the trembling hands, the unnerved limbs, the fading eyes, the same service was exacted as they had rendered in health.

Emily fiercely denied she was ill. Her death should be her own – not put down to some external disease. She refused the family doctor any access to her body. It was hers. Inviolable. *Noli me tangere.*

Emily's 'obstinate fast' touches on what is the burning question with anorexia. Is it a 'condition' (as the attachment 'nervosa' suggests)? Something to be treated? Or is it an act of will, and of self-expression. Something to be respected? In Emily's case, one is led to the latter interpretation.

There are persistent legends (some promulgated by the Haworth 'tat' industry* that Emily 'walks'. Ghosts do not eat. They are fleshless. Incorporeal as well as unreal. Whatever the spectral Cathy is banging on her bedroom window for, it is not porridge (interestingly, though, she has blood, as Lockwood discovers when he scrapes her wrist across the jagged broken glass). Nor, Christian doctrine supposes (Milton goes on about it at some length in Book 5 of *Paradise Lost*), do angels eat. Eating creates rectal filth – there is no sanitation needed in heaven. The

---

* Juliet Barker's contemptuous term (see below, 'Tat', page 156).

damned will not themselves feast in their infernal region, but they can expect to be forever eaten and excreted themselves by the worm.

Reading *Wuthering Heights*, and thinking about its creator, is enough to put you off your food. Or, at least, make you cogitate as you masticate.

OPIUM (1)

Few observations of Marx's are more quoted, and few less understood, than 'Religion is the opium of the people'. It is, in context, a *faute de mieux*, approving comment. Religion is the only painkiller available to the oppressed proletariat. Until revolution. The *mieux*.

Marx made his comment in 1844, around the time that Branwell is first recorded as taking opium. In 1839 he began to eat it (or drink it, as laudanum). He was sometimes bothered by a facial tic, and probably also suffered from epilepsy, and the opium brought some relief. At this period the drug had romantic associations. De Quincey, the famous opium 'eater', and Coleridge, author of 'Kubla Khan', were among Branwell's idols. It was the vice of poets, as TB was the poets' disease. No one could have written 'Kubla Khan' on a bellyful of beer, or 'Ode to a Nightingale' with sound lungs (or, come to that, *Wuthering Heights*). Or so the mythology went.

The young Brontës all devoured the *Confessions of an English Opium Eater*. In various forms opium was available, legally and cheaply, at every corner apothecary and public house. Some bookshops even sold it for their browsing patrons. You could read Mr Coleridge's latest work as high as he was when he wrote it.

Consumption, nationwide, was enormous. Opium was given to babies as soothing medicine and to the dying as painkiller and euphoriant. *Opium* was the opium of the people.

India flooded the English market with the drug as efficiently as (with the aid of British gunboats) it flooded the Chinese market. Its overall effect was tranquillising – it was Prozac, *avant la lettre*, for troubled times. In excess, alcohol provoked ugly violence. No husband beat his wife or children as the result of a lump or two of opium. No child went on a rampage, tearing up the nursery, as the result of a teaspoonful too many of Godfrey's Cordial (the best-known of the narcotic preparations given to infants and children).

The word 'lump', and De Quincey's 'eating' are, however, crucial. Laudanum, one of the favourite means by which opium was ingested, mixed opium and alcohol, in a 90/10 mixture. As Charlotte Brontë astutely observed in *Villette*, too much alcohol, and the multiplier effect of multi-drug intake could be very bad.

Branwell, like many alcoholics, began as a social drinker who, as he became steeped in the stuff, drank over-socially. The old story. What little evidence there is suggests he had a poor head for liquor.

On the rebound from the Robinson imbroglio (see above, 'Branwell's Robinsoniad', page 22) he ran up bills in public houses. In 1846 his drinking debts brought a sheriff's officer to Haworth. Branwell had given his father's name. Either the family paid up, or Branwell would be hauled up in York for debt. Shame all round. The rows which followed are unrecorded. They surely followed.

About the same time he is recorded as using opium, together with alcohol, to ease his suffering, having been shunned by the widowed Mrs Robinson. By 1848, in the months leading up to his death, his intake was, it is suggested, self-destructive, and was aimed to be.

His use of alcohol was always, for the brilliant son of a clergyman (and a thoroughly decent human being), socially degrading. He was letting the family down. How could his father preach temperance, as did his evangelical brethren?

All one needs to know about the later stages of Branwell's drinking career is evident in a letter he wrote to his ally in booze, John Brown, clearly in a state of agonising withdrawal. The note was written on a Sunday, at noon:

> Dear John
> I shall feel very much obliged to you if you can contrive to get me Five pence worth of Gin in a proper measure.
>   Should it be speedily got I could perhaps take it from you or Billy at the lane top.

Brown, one assumes, was being asked to send a boy to the Black Bull, bring back a bottle, and keep a penny for himself.

It's sordid, as is the late career of most drinkers. Branwell could not have it delivered to the house because he was watched there. At night his father slept with him. If one trusts Mrs Gaskell, Branwell would turn in with a knife, his father with his trusty pistol (see below, 'Pistol-Packing Parson', page 131) – albeit one rather disbelieves this nocturnal standoff. One suspects this arrangement may have been for fear that Branwell would choke on his vomit during the night. After one night, he is reported as saying, blurrily, 'The poor old man and I have had a terrible night of it; he does his best – the poor old man! but it's all over with me.'

He probably stole his sixpence for his flagon of mother's ruin (time had passed from the Hogarthian days when it was 'drunk for 1d, dead drunk for 2d, clean straw for nothing'). Branwell, if he got his bottle, would neck the five pennies' worth of gin, splutteringly, in the lane, and stagger back to collapse before the family returned from evensong.

According to the standard account subscribed to by most biographers, Branwell was all this time masking, by inebriation, the TB that actually killed him. Mrs Gaskell, drawing on the scenario relayed to her by Charlotte, writes a gothic account of self-destruction. She had no time for him. He drank alcohol because he was an alcoholic and (as was medical orthodoxy at the time) morally diseased, like all inebriates. But opium, Gaskell suggests, he swallowed massively in his last three years to 'stun his conscience'.

Most addicts (I'm an alcoholic myself)* will wonder about the sketchy outline one has of Branwell Brontë's drinking and drugging, and what look like clear improbabilities in Charlotte's account, which is all the world now has by way of biographical narrative.

Alcoholic self-destruction takes time, access to money, and good supply systems. Incarcerated as he was at Haworth, Branwell would have as much difficulty pickling himself in drink as Dantès in Château d'If (in *The Count of Monte Cristo* – a late 1840s bestseller Branwell might well have looked at, blearily).

'He drank,' says Mrs Gaskell, 'whenever he could get the opportunity.' The opportunities at Haworth parsonage would have been chronically few and far between. Opium presented fewer problems to the abuser because its lumps were 'portable'. Unlike a bottle of gin, they could be secreted – in apertures of the body, if necessary. And the effect was less florid. Given his family

* Non-practising for thirty years.

name, Branwell could 'cajole' (Gaskell's word) the local apothecary to supply him on credit. He displayed, observes Gaskell, 'all the cunning of the opium-eater' in procuring what he needed.

Branwell's death certificate gives as the cause of death 'chronic bronchitis and marasmus [wasting of the body]'. It's not true. It was a combination of drugs and TB that killed him. But, having said that, the accounts left us by Charlotte of his last hours do not ring true.

Two days before his death, Branwell was able to take a walk in the village – an act which does not invoke death throes. The next day he was confined to bed. He answered, obediently and articulately, we are told, to his father's advice on seeking, even at this terminal moment, salvation by true repentance.

On his last evening on earth, in conversation with his gin provider, John Brown, he is reported as crying out: 'In all my past life I have done nothing either great or good. Oh John, I am dying!'

At nine the next morning (a Sunday), we are told, the family (what was left of them) gathered round Branwell's bed. He remained 'perfectly conscious to the end', praying all the while. As he left this life, his last word, as his father prayed, was 'amen'.

There is no doubt he died at Haworth in bed; but anyone who has witnessed a drink-and-drugs death will be suspicious. Nor, in the condition of final collapse, do the terminally tubercular go for country walks 48 hours before expiring. My hunch is that it was, one way or another, suicide – perhaps by self-stored medicine and opium. It would have been a calculated kindness to his family to have eased their misery with a 'good' death.

It takes a lot to make that most level-headed of biographers, Juliet Barker, angry. But in the last paragraph in her great work she turns to denounce Mrs Gaskell for her wilful inconsideration of the son of Haworth:

Branwell's last walk?
The main street in Haworth, at the period the Brontës lived there.

The Branwell who was his family's pride and joy, the
leader and innovator, artist, poet, musician and writer,
is barely touched upon, despite the fact that without
him, there would probably have been no Currer, Ellis,
or Acton Bell.

OPIUM (2)

Mrs Gaskell knew all about opium. The working-class hero of
her first novel, *Mary Barton*, is an addict. Indeed the whole of
working-class Manchester was addicted. As Mrs Gaskell wrote:

> Many a penny that would have gone little way enough
> in oatmeal or potatoes, bought opium to still the hun-
> gry little ones, and make them forget their uneasiness in
> heavy troubled sleep. It was mother's mercy.

As gin was mother's ruin.

Anyone who has read *Villette* will remember Chapter 38,
'Cloud'. The heroine, Lucy Snowe, is given a medicinal dose of
laudanum, to help her sleep through a terrible headache. But too
much alcohol has been put in the potion (perhaps deliberately, by
her rival, Mme Beck). The mixture renders Lucy high as a kite,
and, somnambulistically, she goes wandering, entranced, through
the night-time streets of Brussels.

A fairground Lucy wanders into is a surreal sensory
experience:

> a land of enchantment, a garden most gorgeous, a plain
> sprinkled with coloured meteors, a forest with sparks of

THE POOR CHILD'S NURSE.

A *Punch* cartoon illustrating the uses of opium around this time.

purple and ruby and golden fire gemming the foliage; a
region, not of trees and shadow, but of strangest architec-
tural wealth – of altar and of temple, of pyramid, obelisk,
and sphinx: incredible to say, the wonders and the sym-
bols of Egypt teemed throughout the park of Villette.

A freak-out, as we used to call it in the sixties. Miss Snowe is
tripping. Arguably this is the most accurate, and sympathetic,
description of opiate intoxication in Victorian fiction, until the
degenerates of the fin de siècle came along with their rhapsodies

to hemp, opium, and cocaine. And devoting a chapter to it suggests a more than passing interest on Miss Brontë's part.

Mrs Gaskell, who confessed to having used the stuff herself, was curious.

> I asked her whether she had ever taken opium, as the description given of its effects in *Villette* was so exactly like what I had experienced, — vivid and exaggerated presence of objects, of which the outlines were indistinct, or lost in golden mist, etc. She replied, that she had never, to her knowledge, taken a grain of it.

She had merely 'wondered', Charlotte claimed, about the experience, in bed, before going to sleep. And then dreamed the details. Very realistically, as Mrs G. confirmed.

One is tempted to take it with a grain of something stronger than salt. But the jury is out. And we'll never know and always wonder. The usual situation with the Brontës.

PILLAR

Branwell it was who painted the famous group portrait of Charlotte, Emily and Anne. As a work of art it does not confirm the touching family belief that he was a born genius with the brush. But it demonstrates promise and high teenage competence.

Mrs Gaskell, who saw the painting, declared it 'admirable'. But the picture was marred, as she observed, 'almost in the middle, by a great pillar'.

Gaskell was shown the portrait in 1853. Thereafter it disappeared, and was thought lost. The National Portrait Gallery's

Anne, Emily, large pillar, Charlotte.

notes record that it was found, folded up in quarters on top of a cupboard 'by the second wife of Charlotte Brontë's husband, the Reverend A.B. Nicholls, in 1906'. Why, one wonders, was it put (one might almost say 'thrown') away? Why scrunched up?

The portrait, scarred by its careless folding, was acquired by the gallery and a large simulacrum was painted for the Haworth museum.

Over time, the reason for the pillar has become apparent. As the NPG further notes: 'In the centre of the group a male figure, previously concealed by a painted pillar, can now be discerned; it is almost certainly a self-portrait of the artist, their brother Branwell Brontë.' Custodians at the NPG are said to have observed that, over the decades, Branwell is 'coming through'. Breaking, as it were, through the obscuring pillar.

No other novelists have inspired as many legends about ghosts as the Brontës, and it is tempting to offer up an explanation that continues that tradition. The portrait was done in 1834, internal evidence suggests (such as the gigot sleeves Mrs Gaskell noted, and manifest youthfulness of the sitters.) This was a period when the highest hopes were anticipated for Branwell as an artist. His self-portrait, done by the usual mirror technique, was central. He was the hope of the family. Dominant. But, alas, disgrace ensued. Some hand (all three sisters could draw and paint) 'buried' him, obscurely, behind the pillar. This, perhaps, at the period when the sisters were breaking into print. No embarrassing inquiries about their scapegrace, alcoholic, drug-addicted brother were welcome.

Over the years, a spectral Branwell was forcing his way back into the light. As admirers such as Daphne du Maurier (*The Infernal World of Branwell Brontë*) insist, Branwell has never had his due. He is still fighting for it. Scrabbling, like Cathy at the window in *Wuthering Heights*, to get back (according to du Maurier, he co-wrote that novel).

An alternative view, advanced by Juliet Barker (always ready with a refreshingly sober line of analysis) is that, while painting,

Branwell realised that the composition was too crowded, and obscured himself (with less durable paint). He modestly painted himself out.

Perhaps we may, at last, find out the truth of it. On 18 December 2015 the NPG announced that, as part of the anniversary celebrations, they were going to use state-of-the-art imaging techniques to reveal what lies behind the pillar. Heaven forfend it is the Revd Patrick Brontë.

PISTOL-PACKING PARSON

Patrick Brontë was, like all the English middle classes, much alarmed by the Luddite uprising that swept like wildfire through northern England in the early decades of the 19th century. There was a particularly dangerous outburst of machine wrecking and Captain Swing* mayhem in the West Riding region, where the thirty-something parson (then unmarried) had his first living, at Hartshead (1811–15).

The bloody Luddite attack on the Cartwright mill, at Rawfolds, near Huddersfield, inspired the attack on Moore's mill in *Shirley*. There were assassinations. Patrick proclaimed his loyal anti-Luddite views from the pulpit, and by so doing made himself a prime target. He bought himself a firearm, for personal protection, and carried it with him. This too is recorded in *Shirley*, where the Irish curate, Peter Malone, carries a pistol and shille-lagh with him, even on district visiting to the poor of the parish.

Patrick kept the pistol long after the uprisings were quelled. Mrs Gaskell's passing observation that, even 30 years later, when

---

* The Luddites' mythical leader.

she came on the scene, he was in the habit of discharging the
weapon out of his bedroom window every morning – as some
kind of reveille ritual – has been drawn on as witnessing the
strain of lunacy that ran in the Brontë blood.

It was not, we may deduce, the conventional sidearm. Viz. the
scene in Chapter 13 of *Wuthering Heights*, when Hindley, mad
drunk, tells Nelly his nightly plan to kill Heathcliff:

> 'Look here!' he replied, pulling from his waistcoat a curi-
> ously constructed pistol, having a double-edged spring
> knife attached to the barrel. 'That's a great tempter to a
> desperate man, is it not? I cannot resist going up with
> this every night, and trying his door. If once I find it open
> he's done for! …'
>
> I surveyed the weapon inquisitively. A hideous notion
> struck me: how powerful I should be possessing such
> an instrument! I took it from his hand, and touched
> the blade.

As any historian of 'combination weapons' will tell you, this is an
Unwin & Rodgers. A Sheffield firm, their dual weapons came on
to the market in the early 19th century and proved particularly
salesworthy in Yorkshire at the time of the Luddite alarms.

One can assume that the Brontë children, as mischievous
as they were created, found and played with their father's pistol.
One can assume, too, he often told them about the bloody events,
before their births, of the uprising: hence the episode in *Shirley*.
It had been enshrined in family legend.

There is an innocent explanation for the Revd Brontë's morning discharge. The Unwin & Rodgers was a single-shot weapon.
If the bullet missed, the hope was that you could get your man

with the blade. But once loaded, the 'ball' and powder could not be removed – except by firing. There was no safety catch.

The Luddites had most commonly attacked by night. Before going to bed (having said his prayers and stowed the chamber pot, presumably), Patrick, we may deduce, loaded his gun and put it under his pillow (Nancy Reagan, we are told, did the same with her pearl-handled .38). His single shot out of the window in the morning was to unload the weapon. He did not do his district visiting (in which duty, Mrs Gaskell tells us, he was conscientious) armed to the teeth like Long John Silver. At least, not after 1815. Nor, good father that he was, did he want to leave a loaded gun about the house with children around. Who knows what that wildcat Emily would do with it?

PLAIN JANE

Mrs Gaskell recorded her first impressions of Charlotte Brontë in a private letter, in which she could, as it were, speak plain: 'She is *underdeveloped*, thin and more than half a head shorter than I ... [with] a reddish face, large mouth and many teeth gone; altogether *plain*.'

'Altogether' is a bit hard.

With a defiant 'so be it', Charlotte declared that in *Jane Eyre* she would create 'a heroine as plain and as small as myself'. The name 'Jane' was chosen to echo that resolve. No one, it seems, knows where the phrase 'plain Jane' originates – some accounts think it was popularised in reference to Jane Seymour, the least beautiful of Henry VIII's wives. The phrase received a greater boost from Charlotte's novel, and the reiteration of the epithet in key places of the narrative.

The word 'plain' (bless the e-text's search function) occurs 56 times in *Jane Eyre*, mostly in reference to Jane's unimpressive (to male eyes) appearance.

We no longer use the word 'plain' much, in reference to female facial appearance. The Victorians used it a lot. On the spectrum of female attractiveness plainness is probably central between downright ugly and downright beautiful. It need not, necessarily, it's suggested, put a man off if he looks beneath the surface (fine feathers do not always make fine birds; nor vice versa) to inner worth.

Jane's climactic protest for the rights of the plain woman makes that point passionately:

> 'Do you think, because I am poor, plain, obscure and little, I am soulless and heartless? You think wrong! I have as much soul as you and full as much heart. And if God had gifted me with some beauty and much wealth, I should have made it as hard for you to leave me as it is now for me to leave you. I am not talking to you now through the medium of custom, conventionalities, nor even of mortal flesh – it is my spirit that addresses your spirit; just as if both had passed though the grave, and we stood at God's feet, equal – as we are.'

What is odd is that Jane is not plain when men take note of her. Her inner worth exteriorises itself. She glows. St John's sprightly sister Diana (one of the finer minor characterisations in the novel) makes the point as she urges Jane not to waste herself by marrying her brother and going as a missionary's wife to India:

> 'You do not love him then, Jane?'

'Not as a husband.'

'Yet he is a handsome fellow.'

'And I am so plain, you see, Die. We should never suit.'

'Plain! You? Not at all. You are much too pretty, as well as too good, to be grilled alive in Calcutta.' And again she earnestly conjured me to give up all thoughts of going out with her brother.*

Rochester makes the same point as she prepares for the bridal. Jane, on the pedestal of male desire, is anything but plain.

PRIVACY

There are many oddities about everyday life at Haworth. Most of them, probably, we shall never know about. Among the oddities, for me, is the following episode, recounted in Mrs Gaskell's seminal *The Life of Charlotte Brontë*. As *mise en scène*, recall that Patrick dined alone – why he did so has never been clear. My guess is that he could not stand his children's chatter.

Now, however, when the demand for the work had assured success to 'Jane Eyre,' her sisters urged Charlotte to tell their father of its publication. She accordingly went into his study one afternoon after his early dinner, carrying with her a copy of the book, and one or two reviews, taking care to include a notice adverse to it.

* She should not be doomed to the widow's fate – suttee, burning alive. St John does, in fact, work himself to death in India, after ten years' missionary grind.

She informed me that something like the following conversation took place between her and him. (I wrote down her words the day after I heard them; and I am pretty sure they are quite accurate.)

'Papa, I've been writing a book.'

'Have you, my dear?'

'Yes, and I want you to read it.'

'I am afraid it will try my eyes too much.'

'But it is not in manuscript: it is printed.'

'My dear! You've never thought of the expense it will be! It will be almost sure to be a loss, for how can you get a book sold? No one knows you or your name.'

'But, papa, I don't think it will be a loss; no more will you, if you will just let me read you a review or two, and tell you more about it.'

So she sate down and read some of the reviews to her father; and then, giving him the copy of 'Jane Eyre' that she intended for him, she left him to read it. When he came in to tea, he said, 'Girls, do you know Charlotte has been writing a book, and it is much better than likely?'

It is a quaint and touching scene. But strange. How, one wonders, living as suffocatingly close to each other (and, when it came to consumption, literally suffocatingly) as they all did (one thinks of the three-seater lavatory in the back, and the shared bedding arrangements, between the girls and between Patrick and Branwell), could a father of the household not know that his eldest child (and, as it happened, the other three as well) was writing a three-volume novel?

One of the bitter complaints which Charlotte made about the Héger household was its regime of 'espionage' – everyone sticking their noses into each other's affairs; it was like Bentham's panoptical prison.* But, in the realities of any domestic setting, how could Charlotte *not* know that Emily was writing reams of poetry until she 'accidentally' (one has to suspect snooping) came across her sister's journal? In reconstructing the world of Haworth parsonage, one should imagine bubbles of 'mind your own business!' privacy bumping into each other, but never merging into collectivity.

It has never, I think, been worked out whether, after the communality of childhood Angria/Gondal collaboration, the Brontës critiqued each other's efforts as they were in the process of being written. One thinks probably not. Charlotte so disapproved of *The Tenant of Wildfell Hall*, for example, she would have killed it at birth (as it was, she could only suppress it after Anne died – see below, 'Survivor's Privileges', page 152).

It was, an odd place, Haworth. How can a family have been so close together, yet so separate?

PUBLISHERS

The Prince and the scamp

If there is a heroic publisher in the Brontës' short writing careers there is no question who it was: George Smith the younger (1824–1901), nicknamed the 'Prince of Publishers', for his youth

---

* In the late 18th century, the utilitarian philosopher Jeremy Bentham designed an ideal prison in which prisoners could be observed at all times, even in their cells (George Orwell developed the idea with his 'telescreens' in *Nineteen Eighty-Four*). Bentham's proposal had considerable influence on the later design of prisons.

and precocious brilliance. Less flatteringly he was 'the boy publisher'. He began in his father's firm as an apprentice. The best
snapshot posterity has of him is as 'Doctor John' in *Villette*.

It was Smith who, in 1847, had the wisdom to publish *Jane
Eyre* (and the subsidiary wisdom to reject Charlotte's earlier submitted novel, *The Professor*). Thereafter he nursed her career. She
loved him and the relationship flourished until, to her chagrin,
he chose someone else to marry.

There is, similarly, no question as to who the publishing villain
is in the Brontë chronicles: Thomas Cautley Newby (1797–1882).
It was not merely the sisters whom he exploited: Newby was the
most notorious publisher of fiction in the Victorian period. No
publisher merited more than he Byron's jibe 'now Barabbas was
a publisher'. Charlotte called him 'a shuffling scamp'.

Newby's main line of goods was a steady stream of
three-volume novels for the newly emerging metropolitan
'leviathan libraries' such as, pre-eminently, Mudie's (see below,
'Three-Decker', page 162).

What is remarkable, however, is the impressive list of good
and great novelists who first saw the light of print with Newby's
name and address (72 Mortimer Street) on their title pages: Anne
and Emily Brontë and Anthony Trollope, for example, featured
in his 1847 advertisements. Other novelists whose later distinguished careers he launched (while blandly cheating them) were
Eliza Lynn Linton ('Mr Newby's standing price for first books by
young authors was £50,' she bitterly recorded), Mrs J.H. Riddell
and Julia Kavanagh. He is lampooned, deliciously, in her later
work, *A Struggle for Fame* (1883), as 'Pedland'. Interestingly,
George Smith gets a more favourable portrait as 'Mr P. Vassett'.

Newby was shamelessly dishonest. He capitalised on the
mysterious identity of the author of *Adam Bede* (George Eliot)

by publishing a book supposedly by her. He advertised Anthony Trollope's early works with the implication that they were by his (then) more famous mother, Mrs Frances Trollope.

Newby was Anne and Emily's publisher of last resort. In July 1847 he accepted *Agnes Grey* and *Wuthering Heights* for publication. They were submitted under the sisters' 'Bell' pseudonym. He bundled them together, awkwardly, as a single three-decker.

Having worked out there might be a little money in the Bells' background he demanded a £50 advance payment from the sisters. It was never returned, despite the novels making a profit. He held back publication and then, true to his routine practice, implied in advertisements that the bundle was the work of 'Currer Bell', currently famous for *Jane Eyre*. The trusting Anne nonetheless gave him *The Tenant of Wildfell Hall*, which sold handsomely (across two editions) in summer 1848. Tantalisingly, Emily seems to have been on the way to giving him a successor to *Wuthering Heights*. Charlotte did not, for whatever motives, ease her sisters' way to Smith, Elder & Co.

It took Charlotte, with the aid of George Smith, great effort to recover her dead sisters' copyrights for decent republication under the imprint of Smith, Elder & Co. Charlotte also, surprisingly, managed to screw a small belated payment from Newby.

There is something to be said for the Barabbas of Mortimer Street. He took books other, more reputable publishers had turned down, giving the works a chance to live. Some notable careers were founded on Newby's sharp practice. He had a preference for fiction by women – not merely, perhaps, because they were (like Emily and Anne) more easily exploited. And he advertised widely, with the aim of getting orders from provincial circulating libraries.

Put bluntly: without Newby posterity might not have had two of the masterworks which came from Haworth: *Wuthering Heights* and *The Tenant of Wildfell Hall*. That should earn Thomas Cautley Newby a few days remission from Publishers' Purgatory.

ROCHESTER'S WEALTH

Rochester is a very rich man. He oozes money. But he does not work. He does not even manage the extensive properties he has. He has no 'interests' in the City of London. Where did, and does, the (vast, continuously replenished) Rochester wealth originate?

Not inheritance, at least not immediately. He was a younger son. He explains to Jane what that misfortune means in England, where primogeniture gives all to the eldest (male) offspring:

'… Jane, did you ever hear or know that I was not the eldest son of my house: that I had once a brother older than I?'

'I remember Mrs. Fairfax told me so once.'

'And did you ever hear that my father was an avaricious, grasping man?'

'I have understood something to that effect.'

'Well, Jane, being so, it was his resolution to keep the property together; he could not bear the idea of dividing his estate and leaving me a fair portion: all, he resolved, should go to my brother, Rowland. Yet as little could he endure that a son of his should be a poor man. I must be provided for by a wealthy marriage. He sought me a partner betimes. Mr. Mason, a West India planter and merchant, was his old acquaintance. He was certain his

possessions were real and vast: he made inquiries. Mr.
Mason, he found, had a son and daughter; and he learned
from him that he could and would give the latter a fortune of thirty thousand pounds: that sufficed. When I
left college, I was sent out to Jamaica, to espouse a bride
already courted for me …'

Thirty thousand was, currency conversion informs us, rather
more than a sufficiency. At Thornfield, Jane is probably getting
by on a hundred a year plus bed and board.

Four years later, Rowland, having inherited the Rochester
estate entire, died aged 26, without issue (we don't know how he
died – perhaps dissipation). Edward now found himself the heir.
With, of course, the embarrassment of a mad wife (her thirty
thousand remained his, of course). He now had money enough to
deal with that problem; although locking her with a drunk keeper
in an upstairs room was one of the cheaper options.

The Rochester wealth, we can confidently presume (they
and the Masons are 'old acquaintances'), came from the same
source as that of Bertha's family. Slave-worked sugar plantations
in Jamaica, that is, in the British West Indies. The action of *Jane
Eyre* is set (although it slithers a bit – *see above* 'Dates', page 43)
in the 1820s, some years before the final abolition of slavery in
the islands in 1833.

Rochester is heir to wealth generated by black sweat and
brutality in distant sugar fields over hundreds of years. Late in
the novel Jane herself becomes an heiress – to a fortune made
by her (distant) family in Madeira. How was colonial wealth
generated there? From sugar, rum and the dessert wine named
after the island. How, historically, were those crops gathered and
refined into delectable liquor. By slave labour – who did not, on

the whole, take a glass of Madeira, my dear, after their evening meal. Jane's wealth too has an origin some readers may not want to think about as they rejoice in her 'liberation'.

Jane Eyre ends in leafy Ferndean. No couple is happier than the Rochesters. Neither of them work. No need. Their slaves do it for them. They have done for aeons. Pull that rope, tote that bale.

SELF-MURDER

For most of Christianity's rule in Britain suicide was thus described. There is a relevant exchange between Nelly and Heathcliff on the subject. She has deduced that he intends to kill himself by starvation and remonstrates:

> 'And supposing you persevered in your obstinate fast, and died by that means, and they refused to bury you in the precincts of the kirk?' I said, shocked at his godless indifference. 'How would you like it?'

Heathcliff's reply is very *Wuthering Heights*:

> 'They won't do that,' he replied: 'if they did, you must have me removed secretly; and if you neglect it you shall prove, practically, that the dead are not annihilated!'

He will, he threatens, come back and haunt her. It's a shrewd threat. Nelly, like Tabitha Aykroyd with her belief in 'fairies' (see above, 'Ghosts', page 53), has a peasant fear of the undead. But the notion of her exhuming, by shovel, Heathcliff's mouldering corpse, having pulled out the stake nailing the suicide to the earth (see below), and then lugging it to the consecrated ground of Gimmerton Kirk for clandestine, non-Christian burial, in Christian earth, is a stretch.

There is a clear hint of self-murder in both the principals' deaths. Villagers ignorant of the circumstances of Catherine's death (and supposing it to have been due to the rigours of childbirth – common enough) are taken aback when they see where she is buried: ambiguously in the margin of sacred and non-sacred earth:

> The place of Catherine's interment, to the surprise of the villagers, was neither in the chapel under the carved monument of the Lintons, nor yet by the tombs of her own relations, outside. It was dug on a green slope in a corner of the kirk-yard, where the wall is so low that heath and bilberry-plants have climbed over it from the moor; and peat-mould almost buries it.

Suicide remained a crime in England until 1961, incredibly and shamefully. There are still, as late as 2016, bars in the way of full Christian obsequies for suicides.

The interment regulations in the 19th century were positively medieval. If suicide were proved, the corpse was taken, by night, to a crossroads, buried in a hole without marker or ceremony, with a stake through the body (resurrection was thus prevented – a cruel posthumous punishment, like the quicklime thrown on the bodies of executed murderers).

Until 1822 (twenty years before the main action of *Wuthering Heights*), a suicide's possessions could be forfeit to the crown. Crossroad burial was abolished at the same period. Macadamized roads were one reason. Patrick Brontë must, charitably, have dealt with the self-murdered, and given them illicit rest in Haworth churchyard. One hopes so. From what one knows of him (thanks to the rescue efforts of Juliet Barker) he was a kind man.

Two of Patrick's children, Emily and Branwell (see above, 'Obstinate Fasting', page 116; and 'Opium [1]', page 120) could plausibly be thought to have 'murdered' themselves. They lie, peacefully, in the family vault; not, as they should be, 200 yards away in the unhallowed earth of the Church Lane/West Lane crossroads.

SPIRIT-WRITTEN

'There are stories,' the anonymous blogger on the lively 'Ghost Cities' site* reports,

> that, after Emily's death in 1848, she appeared to her last remaining sister Charlotte with her last unpublished work. This so-called 'lost Brontë' is said to still be out there somewhere, perhaps buried in the churchyard at Haworth. Emily's ghost is doomed to wander the moors – much like her heroine Catherine – until this is found and published.

That there may have been a second novel under way when Emily died, on 19 December 1848, is given currency by a letter written by her rogue of a publisher, T.C. Newby. What Newby wrote to 'Ellis Bell' on 15 February 1848 is tantalising:

> I am much obliged by your kind note and shall have great pleasure in making arrangements for your next novel.

* One of many such sites – most informative.

I would not hurry its completion, for I think you are quite right not to let it go before the world until well satisfied with it, for much depends on your new work. If it be an improvement on your first, you will have established yourself as a first rate novelist, but if it fall short the Critics will be too apt to say that you have expended your talent in your first novel. I shall therefore have pleasure in accepting it upon the understanding that its completion be in your own time.

If only the fool had asked her to make all speed, as did George Smith with *Jane Eyre*. Time was the one thing Emily Brontë did not have. But the idea of a second novel already under way would seem, on the face of it, a strong possibility. Clearly the proposal for a follow-up came from her. How far ahead with thinking and writing did Emily come in the eight months remaining to her on earth? Were preparatory materials destroyed with the other literary remains Charlotte is accused of having destroyed, after her sisters' deaths?

The brain spins. What subject would Emily – a novelist developing at lightning speed artistically – have moved on to? A sequel? A 'factory' novel (there were many small industrial firms in Haworth and the 'workshop of the world', Manchester, was not far away)? A novel on Liverpool's slave trade?

Wonder no more. On 30 October 2014 the *Keighley News* (located not too far from Haworth) ran a story under the eye-catching headline: "'Ghost writer" claims she has penned Emily Brontë's missing second novel'. It opened:

Emily Brontë's 'lost' novel has been published after she communicated from the grave with a modern-day writer.

This is the claim of Leeds woman Morwenna Holman, who says she collaborated with the ghost of the famous author of *Wuthering Heights*.

'Spirit writer' Morwenna last year published *Westerdale* after many hours speaking with 'real perfectionist' Emily and has gone on to write a sequel entitled *Heaton*.

A third novel, no less. Roam no more Emily.

Ms Holman claimed to have been in communication with Emily since visiting the museum and vault, aged ten. She was not frightened by the novelist's visitations: she (Ms Holman) had been seeing spirits 'since about the age eight'.

She was not yet, however, ready for the full blast of extra-sensory communication from the author, who had selected her as her posthumous outlet. 'At the age of 18 my psychic powers reached their full strength,' she complacently records, 'and Emily told me I had to write her second novel, which was destroyed by Charlotte when she lay dying.'

Westerdale is available from Olympia Press, kindled by Amazon for a very appealing price. It chronicles, like *Wuthering Heights*, a struggle between two 'houses', with a moorland setting. Emily was not yet ready, we apprehend, to change her formula. For those who purchase the novel, Ms Holman adds:

> I run a small cat rescue for abandoned felines and every penny of the royalty money for my books will be going to the rescue.

Westerdale is (in my estimation) an interesting read. More so since 'spirit writing' – a small, strange genre – is itself an interesting phenomenon, witnessing to the power great writers have over us. They 'capture' us.

Spirit communication with great dead is, in general, safer ground than ghost-writing, secretarially, new literary master-works from ghosts. Victor Hugo, one is told, claimed to chat with Moses, Jesus, Mohammed and Martin Luther, inter alia. What they said, he did not divulge. His fiction tells the tale.

Attempts to channel actual literary works (or musical works) by geniuses, usually via the Ouija board, or *planchette*, are relatively rare – and never successful since the results can be compared, to their inevitable detriment, with what was written while the authors were still alive and kicking. Take, for example (leaving *Westerdale* to one side) *Jap Heron* (1917) by Emily Grant Hutchings and 'Mark Twain'. It has the frank subtitle, 'A novel written via the Ouija board'. Hutchings discovered she had been recruited as Twain's 'pencil on earth'. She was sued on earth by the Twain estate, unimpressed by the Ouija board, and *Jap Heron* disappeared. It's now available online. And, as with *Westerdale*, alas (one feels for the cats), one feels that, wherever they find themselves for eternity, great writers should observe silence after death. Poor Emily, one suspects, is doomed to wander the moors forever.

STEEL

In his 1855 poetic reflections in the graveyard at Haworth (a poem which laid the foundations for much of the subsequent hyper-romantic Brontë legend), Matthew Arnold describes Anne's genius as the least 'puissant' of the sisters'. Odd word.

Anne is also regarded as the most submissive Brontë sister.

And the most reticent personally. There was, said Charlotte, in a much-quoted obituary piece on her two writing sisters, a 'nun-like veil' which covered her feelings and 'was rarely lifted'. Even to the family, apparently. Was there ever a more opaque end to a novel than that to *Agnes Grey*: 'And now I think I have said sufficient'? No you haven't, Agnes! the reader thinks.

There was, as Charlotte observed, a certain 'obduracy' in Anne's character and, as her most sympathetic biographers (notably Winifred Gerin) have claimed, a vein of inner 'steel' in her personality. What, then, is that steely quality?

A picture of Anne, which captures the willpower
underlying her docile exterior.

It helps to approach the question from an oblique angle. In an article entitled '"Hapless Dependents": Women and Animals in Anne Brontë's *Agnes Grey*', published in the learned journal *Studies in the Novel* (2002), Maggie Berg opens with a declaration of pedagogic perplexity:

> In one of my recent graduate classes on the Brontës, the presenter of *Agnes Grey* [i.e. the student reading out their class assignment] observed as an amused aside that the whole moral scheme of the novel seemed to revolve around how animals are treated. The class laughed derisively.

Professor Berg was not amused. The reaction of her students made her think about Anne and animals and this strange theme in the novel.

In simple narrative terms the student's comment is true. Animals, domestic and wild, feature centrally in the novel. One animal, the dog Snap, has a starring role, running in tandem with that of his eventual mistress.

A 'little rough terrier', Snap comes into Agnes's possession, from a negligent and cruel owner, in her second governess post. She looks after him from infancy to adolescence. He turns out to be a very lovable adult dog. Only Agnes shows him the love he responds to. But, like Agnes, his place in the family is precarious. Like her, he has the Damoclean sword – dismissal – over his head. It inevitably falls:

> Snap, my little dumb, rough-visaged, but bright-eyed, warm-hearted companion, the only thing I had to love me, was taken away, and delivered over to the tender

mercies of the village rat-catcher, a man notorious for his brutal treatment of his canine slaves.

Snap drops out of the story until, as Agnes is walking her beloved (Scarborough) sands:

> I heard a snuffling sound behind me and then a dog came frisking and wriggling to my feet. It was my own Snap – the little dark, wire-haired terrier! When I spoke his name, he leapt up in my face and yelled for joy. Almost as much delighted as himself, I caught the little creature in my arms, and kissed him repeatedly. But how came he to be there? He could not have dropped from the sky, or come all that way alone: it must be either his master, the rat-catcher, or somebody else that had brought him; so, repressing my extravagant caresses, and endeavouring to repress his likewise, I looked round, and beheld – Mr. Weston!

It is the curate she loves who has rescued him. The jointly loved dog seals their union, each of the three loving the others forever and ever.

It is sentimental, of course. The brutally unsentimental scenes in the novel are those in which the abominable man-child Tom tortures any animal that comes his way, looking forward impatiently to his adult manhood when he can whip ('cut' horses) mercilessly, and shoot and torment anything furred and feathered. He is not a hunter but a sadist. And typical of his whip- and gun-wielding gender.

Agnes's womanhood rebels against Tom's cruelty to animals. Her rebellion goes beyond protest. In the most horrific scene in the novel she acts with defiant resolve. The scene opens with Tom running into the Bloomfield garden 'in high glee' with 'a brood of little callow nestlings' in his hands. His sisters (Agnes's charges) want to nurse the chicks. But Tom has other plans, 'laying the nest on the ground, and standing over it with his legs wide apart, his hands thrust into his breeches-pockets'.

He wears the trousers. He will shock and awe the womenfolk by 'fettling 'em off. My word, but I will wallop 'em? See if I don't now. By gum! but there's rare sport for me in that nest.' Master Tom will show who is master.

Agnes tells him she will not let him torture the birds. They must be taken back, she says, to where their nest came from. If he won't tell her where that is, 'I shall kill them myself – much as I hate it.' She can't, Tom commands her. She's a servant. He's a master. But do it she does, even if it means losing her position:

> So saying – urged by a sense of duty – at the risk of both making myself sick and incurring the wrath of my employers – I got a large flat stone, that had been reared up for a mouse-trap by the gardener; then, having once more vainly endeavoured to persuade the little tyrant to let the birds be carried back, I asked what he intended to do with them. With fiendish glee he commenced a list of torments; and while he was busied in the relation, I dropped the stone upon his intended victims and crushed them flat beneath it.

His uncle comes up and supports Tom in his violence. It's a man thing: 'He's beyond petticoat government already: by God! he defies mother, granny, governess, and all!'

What is striking in this scene is the pitting of male against female. It is not, principally, about kindness or cruelty to animals; rather, it is proto-feminism that one sees in Agnes's defiance against the little tyrant. And male chauvinism in what Tom is doing. The contest is explicitly political.

The early energies of the Victorian women's movement were kindled, and mobilised, by protest against male treatment of the 'lesser creation' – a description which fitted women as much as animals. The notable pioneer of rights for women Frances Power Cobbe was, for example, a founder of the Victoria Street Society for the Protection of Animals Liable to Vivisection. The Royal Society for the Prevention of Cruelty to Animals bore the warrant of the most powerful woman in the world (who was notably kind to animals).

Anne did not live long enough to join the anti-vivisection, women's rights movement. She would have been in its forefront, fighting the universal Toms of the world: the 'tyrant sex'. Therein lies Anne Brontë's inner steel.

SURVIVOR'S PRIVILEGES

One knows infuriatingly little about the day-to-day relations between the sisters. One of the things which is clear is that, at least in her later years, when her religious views hardened, Charlotte took an increasingly dim view of both Anne's and Emily's fiction. Disapproved, in fact, to the extent of actively suppressing rather than promoting it.

After the deaths of the younger Brontës the noble George Smith, who had acquired the Acton/Ellis copyright, suggested, in summer 1850, that Smith, Elder reissue them, properly, textually corrected, 'with a prefatory and explanatory notice of the authors'.

Wuthering Heights and *Agnes Grey* were duly reissued, in a combined edition (as they had customarily been packaged) prefaced by a 'biographical notice of Ellis and Acton Bell by Charlotte Brontë'. *The Tenant of Wildfell Hall*, however, was kept out of print (almost certainly at Charlotte's request) for some years.

In that 'prefatory and explanatory notice' Charlotte is damning in her verdict on 'Acton's' second novel, declaring that, in her judgement, Anne/Acton had been defeated as an artist by a subject entirely beyond her powers:

> She had, in the course of her life, been called on to contemplate near at hand, and for a long time, the terrible effects of talents misused and faculties abused; hers was a naturally sensitive, reserved and dejected nature; what she saw sank very deeply into her mind: it did her harm. She brooded over it till she believed it to be a duty to reproduce every detail (of course, with fictitious characters, incidents and situations), as a warning to others.

The Tenant of Wildfell Hall is, posterity has come to believe, something more than a temperance tract by a woman traumatised by the proximity of a drunk in the family. Why talk down the novel in this way?

In the same preface Charlotte's comments seem to misread, caricature even, what Emily achieved. The novel was, she wrote: 'hewn in a wild workshop, with simple tools, out of homely materials', 'moorish, and wild, and knotty as a root of heath'.

The 'wild workshop' comment (implying she humped her escritoire, pen and ink with her on long moorland walks) echoes Victor Frankenstein, creating his monster:

I collected bones from charnel-houses; and disturbed, with profane fingers, the tremendous secrets of the human frame. In a solitary chamber, or rather cell, at the top of the house, and separated from all the other apartments by a gallery and staircase, I kept *my workshop of filthy creation*. [my italics]

Her sister, too, Charlotte said, had created a monster: 'Whether it is right or advisable to create beings like Heathcliff, I do not know: I scarcely think it is.' The appended clause has a scorpion sting to it.

Smith, Elder requested portraits of Anne and Emily, to be included in the volume. It would be clinching proof of the 'Bell' sisters' existence, in the (female) flesh. The family had, Charlotte 'grieved' to say, by way of reply, 'no portrait of either of my sisters'. The editor of her letters, Margaret Smith, notes that there were portraits aplenty. Charlotte wanted only one available to the world: the flattering picture (*opposite*) that George Smith had commissioned from George Richmond, in the same year, 1850.

This picture was important to her. George Smith, who paid for it, observed that no woman wanted more to be pretty than Charlotte – who wasn't. The picture is, undeniably, of a pretty woman. One recalls Mrs Gaskell's description of her first meeting with Charlotte:

Presently the door opened, and in came a superannuated mastiff, followed by an old gentleman very like Miss Brontë, who shook hands with us, and then went to call his daughter. A long interval, during which we coaxed the old dog, and looked at a picture of Miss Brontë, by Richmond, the solitary ornament of the room, looking

George Richmond's portrait of Charlotte Brontë.
Commissioned by George Smith, it was, one may surmise,
the finest compliment ever paid Charlotte.

strangely out of place on the bare walls, and at the books
on the little shelves, most of them evidently the gift of
the authors since Miss Brontë's celebrity.

One could see Charlotte's handling of the introduction of her
sisters to the world as intended to generate a kind of protective
mystique. A dry ice effect. Or something intended to background them in the general enterprise of their joint creation.

It's a question which continues to perplex Brontë scholars. How 'nice' a sister was Charlotte?

TAT

That three-letter word is what Juliet Barker calls Haworth's commercial homage to the Brontës, the family who have made their little town (now without the industry that it once had) world-famous. On the same theme, John Barlow makes merry with the town's wholesale Brontëfication:

> In the small Yorkshire village of Haworth, where the Brontë sisters lived quietly with their clergyman father while penning some of the greatest novels in the English language, there are road signs in Japanese. Walk down the stone-cobbled main street, which looks much as it did two centuries ago (minus the blood-stained phlegm of the consumptives) and you can buy Brontë biscuits and gingerbread, Brontë fleeces, and Brontë flagstones (for your literary-themed driveway). You might then want to take refreshment at the *Villette* Coffee House (*Villette*, the novel by Charlotte they don't even force you to read at school), before stocking up on Brontë tea-towels – just impossible to get in Osaka. The Brontë Hairdressing Salon salvages some local pride by refusing to call itself Jane Hair (at least two salons in neighbouring towns, though, are guilty), and the Brontë Balti House is there for all your literary-themed curry needs.*

---

* John Barlow, *Everything but the Squeal* (2008).

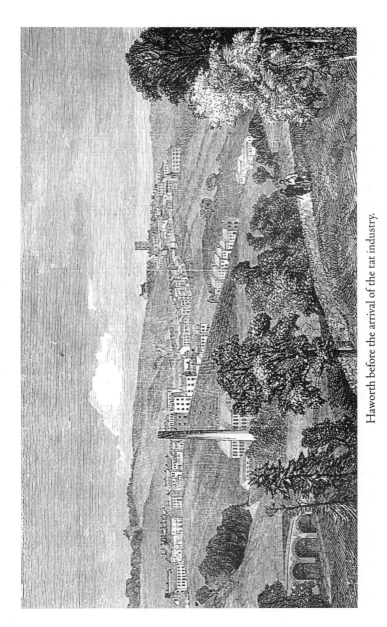

Haworth before the arrival of the tat industry.

It's scornful. And funny. But one could – tongue in cheek – mount a perverse defence arguing for the worthwhileness of tat. Personally I find 'Jane Hair' no more offensive than the 1980 'Famous Authoress' series of postage stamps, in which Charlotte Brontë looked like Charlotte Brontë as reconstructed long after the decompositions of death by an Egyptian embalmer who hadn't quite learned his trade. Her fellow authoresses looked no better. But licking the back-side of those ladies' images meant some apology for all the male tongues which had disrespected them over the years.

And there are, of course, those purists who think the TV and film adaptations of the Brontës' works are a kind of impurification. Myself, I have always had a soft spot for the ghostly Heathcliff (Laurence Olivier) and Cathy (Merle Oberon) skipping over Penistone Crags (recognisably the San Gabriels, a conveniently short drive from the Hollywood Goldwyn Studio – I've skipped those hills myself). I can keep the images separate from the novel.

I personally have always enjoyed, when in the US, Lorna Doone biscuits, munching away with thoughts of Jan and Carver doing battle. I love the literary-themed hotels which advertised their comforts around the old British Library, in Victorian Bloomsbury. There was the homage-to-Thackeray Esmond Hotel (Charlotte would have stayed there). The Kingsley (named after the author of *Westward Ho!*) is still there, but has recently been renamed The Thistle. The Kenilworth is still there under its 150-year-old name. Few, alas, read Scott's novel any more. But Emily was a great lover of the Wizard of the North. His *The Black Dwarf* is one of *Wuthering Heights*' source-novels.

Three Castles cigarettes were promoted as a Thackeray-endorsed product, with a quotation from *The Virginians* on every packet. Dickens, known to be prone to the pesky things, has had his picture on a piles (haemorrhoids) ointment advertisement. That may be, I grant, a commercial exploitation too far.

One could go on. There are, as John Barlow notes, any number of Brontë themed shelf-wares nowadays. My favourite is a 'Wuthering Heights Soy Candle' by bookish candle maker The Melting Library. I think I can pick out 'Heather and Fresh Rain' on the label. The nostrils quiver, approvingly.

Charlotte's signature novel has always been attractive to soft-pornographers. There is a *Jane Eyrotica*, a *Jane Eyre Laid Bare* … a 'Clandestine Classics' version of *Jane Eyre*, adapted by one Sierra Cartwright, also contains departures from Charlotte's text: the advertisement recounts how 'Jane has passionate sex with Mr Rochester before leaving him'. Ho hum.

There is no fate worse for fiction than to come and go into Shakespeare's 'wallet for oblivion'. Everything from 'Jane Hair' salons to *Jane Eyrotica* confirms that will never happen to the Brontës' fiction. Their novels will last for as long as there is money to be made from the novels, which are wholly uncontaminated. Long live 'tat': it bears witness to long life.

TEETHING

Judged purely by his actions, Heathcliff is an utter swine: a wife-beater, child-abuser, card-sharp and, I maintain, a murderer.* Why, then do we forgive his crimes and demonic cruelty and admire him, and concur when Laurence Olivier (and, my God, Cliff Richard) plays him as a heroic figure?

* See *Is Heathcliff a Murderer?* (1996)

An explanation for the 'sympathy for the devil' paradox ('devil daddy', mini-Heathcliff calls him) is to be found, I suggest, in a muttered ejaculation overheard by Nelly, Wuthering Heights' ever-ready Keyhole Kate, in the extremity of Heathcliff's grief and sexual frustration after Cathy's death:

> I have no pity! I have no pity! The [more the] worms writhe, the more I yearn to crush out their entrails! It is a *moral teething*, and I grind with greater energy, in proportion to the increase of pain. [my italics]

The reason for our (perverse) sympathy for Heathcliff, I suggest, is to be found in that arresting phrase, 'moral teething' and what it implies to any parent or other observer of babies who has seen them undergo their first dentition: the arrival of their 'milk teeth'.

When a baby savagely bites its teething ring (or some other handy object – a parent's finger?) it is because baby is experiencing excruciating pain from the teeth tearing their way through the gums. So Heathcliff may be seen to inflict pain on others (blacking his wife's eyes, striking young Catherine, lashing his horses and dogs) only because he feels greater pain himself. He suffers more than he inflicts. Pity the poor fellow. But keep out of the demon's way.

THAT NAME

The most resonant surname in women's fiction of the mid-19th century is also the strangest. It originates with a remarkable father: a man whose life achievements are, unfairly, one might think, eclipsed by the brilliance of his children.

One of ten children of a farming family, he had been born Patrick Prunty. The name is common to this day in Co. Down, Northern Ireland, where it is sometimes given the chauvinistic Celtic spelling, O'Pronteaigh. As a child he was probably called 'Paddy'.

Patrick was born in the region, on St Patrick's Day, 1777, of mixed Protestant and Catholic parentage. He gave early evidence of an exceptionally quick mind. It led, by the hardest of educational routes, to the young Irishman's registering in 1802 at Cambridge University with a view to ordination in the Church of England. Pruntys were not common in that institution. A different throw of the dice, following his other parent (his mother, one assumes), and he might have become a Catholic priest.

There were historical problems with the name 'Patrick Prunty' – a name which had the same sinister resonances with English congregations as, say, 'Gerry Adams', or 'Martin McGuinness' would have (before they went respectable) 200 years later. In 1798 there had been a bloody uprising in Ireland led by the 'Society of United Irishmen', egged on by France (currently at war with England). Ireland and the Irish were not trusted, or liked, by the English middle classes in 1802. At this period, Patrick prudently (given his future career in the Church of England) renamed himself 'Brontë'.

The diaeresis, or umlaut, provided further distance from his Hibernian origins. It was, and is, a mark associated with Germany, not Ireland, a country where umlauts are as rare as the venomous snakes which St Patrick banished from the island. The name is sometimes given a terminal French acute accent – but, as has been said, that nation was not universally loved in England during the Napoleonic Wars.

There are two suggested reasons for the Revd Brontë's choice of his new name. The word is an anglicisation of the ancient Greek for 'thunder', which, with his newly acquired classical learning, may have tickled the young Cantab's scholarly *amour-propre*. The more plausibly suggested reason is patriotism – to England, that is, not Ireland. Admiral Lord Nelson had been appointed Duke of Brontë in 1799 by Ferdinand, King of the Two Sicilies and Infante of Spain, grateful for the nautical hero's exploits against Napoleon. Short of renaming himself 'the Revd John Bull', Patrick could not have decontaminated himself more effectively from any disloyal Hibernian affiliation.

One should, in conscience, note Juliet Barker's less florid explanation, originating in Patrick's registration, in October 1802, at St John's College, Cambridge:

> He had an inauspicious start to his new life. Defeated by his Irish accent the registrar attempted a phonetic spelling of the name he gave, entering 'Patrick Branty' in the admissions book … two days later … he did not allow it to go unchallenged and the entry was altered from 'Branty' to the now famous 'Brontë'.

I prefer the Greek explanation. It is, somehow, more 'Brontëan'.

THREE-DECKER

The cable channel Netflix, it was suggested in 2016, has created new modes and habits of TV-narrative viewing. The assertion revolves around a regular controversy: particle issue versus whole story consumption.

Long narratives, such as, pre-eminently, *Breaking Bad* and *The Wire*, were delivered to cable-subscribing viewers as weekly serial parts. Netflix then introduced long narratives, such as *House of Cards* (or, on Amazon Prime, *The Man in the High Castle*) whose dozen or so instalments could be 'binge watched': non-stop, hour after hour.

Which form worked best? The 'make 'em laugh, make 'em cry, make 'em *wait*' serial issue, advocated by Wilkie Collins (Victorian master of the fragmented narrative and delayed revelation)? Or the 'single lump' narrative, swallowed whole, as a boa constrictor swallows a living goat?

As regards Victorian fiction there were the monthly/weekly serialists (predominantly Dickens) and those who produced their works entire, in volume form. George Eliot serialised masterfully. If one can discipline oneself, it is worth reading *Middlemarch*, with monthly breaks, over three-quarters of a year. Reading, that is, like a Victorian of 1871–2.

Charlotte Brontë was very much of the boa constrictor party. The wisest words ever spoken to her, as regards the marketing of her fiction, were George Smith's writing (in the letter rejecting *The Professor*) that his firm would be very interested in receiving a *three-volume* novel from her. The fact that *The Professor* could only be stretched to two volumes was one of the reasons for not wanting it.

Overlong (up to 250,000 words at its most bloated), over-priced (at a guinea-and-a-half), and almost from the first overdue for extinction, the 'three-decker' began with Walter Scott in 1819 and saw out Thomas Hardy's novel-writing career in the 1890s. Every one of the Brontë sisters' novels, when first published in their lifetimes, came out in three volumes.*

---

* Emily's and Anne's publisher Thomas Newby concocted a faux three-decker by bundling *Wuthering Heights* and *Agnes Grey* together as a chalk-and-cheese package (see 'Publishers', page 137).

The reason the three-decker lasted so long was that it coincided with the circulating library system. During the 1840s there emerged two 'leviathans': Mudie's, based in London, and W.H. Smith, operating via the arterial railway system. Three-deckers meant that Mudie's talismanic subscription model, where a guinea entitled you to unlimited loans for a year – but only one volume at a time – could satisfy three different customers simultaneously.

It involved the suspenseful 'waiting' Collins described. If a family shared a single subscription – as they often did – a reader might have to wait for several family members to finish with the coveted next volume before getting their turn. There were, doubtless, spoiler alerts over the breakfast table.

One of the remarkable things about Charlotte was not that she produced *Jane Eyre* fast – although she did: in months – but that she grasped, intuitively, the ideal internal architecture of the three-decker.

Handling the form well entailed three climaxes – hitting the reader like cresting, crashing waves. The first volume of *Jane Eyre* ends with one of its most dramatic scenes. Jane cannot sleep. She hears a strange laugh and smells smoke. She goes to Rochester's bedroom (normally an inviolable space for a maiden). His bed hangings are on fire. She takes the ewer and basin, put out for his morning's ablutions, and douses the flames. He wakes and thanks his 'cherished' preserver. She returns to her virginal couch:

> but never thought of sleep. Till morning dawned I was
> tossed on a buoyant but unquiet sea, where billows of
> trouble rolled under surges of joy. I thought sometimes
> I saw beyond its wild waters a shore, sweet as the hills of
> Beulah; and now and then a freshening gale, wakened by

hope, bore my spirit triumphantly towards the bourne:
but I could not reach it, even in fancy – a counteract-
ing breeze blew off land, and continually drove me back.
Sense would resist delirium: judgment would warn passion. Too feverish to rest, I rose as soon as day dawned.

Who did it? What is going on at Thornfield? The reader's mind
runs wild.

The second volume's last chapter begins with the happy peal
of wedding bells. It ends, after the discovery of Bertha, with
another great question: will Jane remain as Rochester's mistress?
Or leave – where, to do what? Hands twitch to get hold of the
third volume, in which everything will be revealed. And the third
climax? Reader, I married him.

The narrative dynamism of the three-decker is something we
have lost. Sadly, in my view.

TOOTHSOME

Among Mrs Gaskell's first observations of Charlotte Brontë,
along with her short stature and 'reddish face', is that she had
'many teeth gone'. That Emily had a disfiguringly protruding front
tooth is one of the very few facts we know about her (that and
the fact that she was measured at five foot seven when fitted for
her coffin. A tall woman by Brontë standards).

Teeth glint (or not) from time to time in the fiction – usually with significant stress. Young Martin's saucy comments to
Caroline Helstone in *Shirley*, for example (there is evidence
that Caroline is a fictional depiction of Anne), is pure Colgate
advertisement:

'You may laugh: I have no objection to see you laugh:
your teeth – I hate ugly teeth; but yours are as pretty as
a pearl necklace, and a necklace, of which the pearls are
very fair, even, and well matched too.'

We don't know about Miss Eyre's teeth. But the grand ladies
clustered around la belle Ingram, her rival, attract the following
comment:

They were all three of the loftiest stature of women. The
Dowager might be between forty and fifty: her shape was
still fine; her hair (by candle-light at least) still black; her
teeth, too, were still apparently perfect.

'Apparently'? Are they false? We are led to be suspicious. Who
has white teeth at fifty?

Joseph, that age, presumably, is as toothless as the hens
clucking in the coops outside Wuthering Heights. Or, at least,
so we may assume from the old bigot's mumbling, his dyspepsia
and his invariable diet of porridge. But Heathcliff's teeth are
manifestly in extraordinarily good shape for someone of his
age (39 when we first meet him) and class background. A
'slovenly squire', Lockwood calls him. In his youth he was a
stable boy – munching porridge from the same pot as Joseph.
Heathcliff is routinely described during the course of the narrative as grinding, clenching and gnashing his teeth. They are,
clearly, in excellent gnashing fettle. The fact could be thought
strange.

That Heathcliff goes to the grave, and his hyperactive after-
life, with a perfect set of gnashers in his jaw is disclosed in Nelly's
recollection to Lockwood of finding his emaciated corpse at the

window where he has starved to death, waiting, until death do them join, for his spectral love, Cathy.

> I hasped the window; I combed his black long hair from his forehead; I tried to close his eyes: to extinguish, if possible, that frightful, life-like gaze of exultation before any one else beheld it. They would not shut: they seemed to sneer at my attempts; and his parted lips and sharp white teeth sneered too!

How, one may wonder, has Heathcliff contrived to keep his 'sharp white teeth' in such Tom Cruise-like condition? Is this proof of his 'vampirism' (see below, 'Vampirology [1]', page 173)?

There are more mundane explanations. He learned many things, we may deduce, in his three lost years, returning, as he did, a well-spoken 'gentleman' with a foreign accent and money in his purse. One important thing he may well have learned was how gentlemen cared for their teeth.

Sponges dipped in aromatic fluid were what Lord Chesterfield, that *arbiter elegantiarum*, advocated (it sweetened the breath, which the ladies liked). There were also dentifrice powders (the poor used, if anything, chimney dust). Handled brushes, of the kind we are familiar with, were used by the genteel classes – particularly women.

A utensil much in favour with gentlemen was the tooth-brush and razor set, sold by jewellers or high-class barbers. They would contain, in an elegant (goatskin-coated) box, brushes, a tooth powder recess, and a tongue scraper. And, of course, an open razor.

The point is stressed that on his return, the 'transformed' Heathcliff has learned the gentlemanly use of the razor during his three years' absence. On first catching sight of his face Nelly notes that his cheeks are 'half covered with black whiskers'. Other male residents of Wuthering Heights, we gather from Lockwood's appalled description, have shaggy beards. Hareton's whiskers, for example, 'encroach bearishly over his cheeks'.

And, of course, gentlemen, alone and in male company, would always have to hand, in their waistcoat pockets, their toothpicks (often metal; sometimes precious metal). These instruments would appear, along with cigars and chamber pots behind screens, when the ladies 'retired', after dinner, and the men could 'untruss'; and tell smoking room stories, while they scraped their ivories. Dickens's toothpick, with ivory and gold decorations, was sold for $9,000 at auction in 2009. Lovers of *Jurassic Park* will wonder if any DNA remained on it, wherewith future science might recreate the Great Inimitable. Dream on.

All of this by way of explanation of Heathcliff's dentition. But why, one may ask, were Charlotte's teeth so rotted? My guess is that the Brontës (at least the ladies) would have had one shared toothbrush, as they also had one face flannel and towel over their bedroom bowls and pitchers. They looked after their teeth.

But one deduces, from scraps of evidence, that Charlotte had more trouble with her teeth than her grown siblings. I am neither a dentist nor a physician but I think the reason may have been her chronic ill-health and the 'blue pill' she took by way of remedy. Blue pills were prescribed for every ailment: minor and major, from syphilis to constipation. Their active ingredient was mercury.

There was, in 19th-century Britain and America, a secret epidemic of mercury poisoning as a result of this popular, toxic, medication. The long-term, overdose symptoms were depression, insomnia and fits of mental instability – even madness (mercury does terrible things to the brain and nervous system). And loose teeth. Loose enough to be pulled out at home, by the owners themselves. It's as good an explanation as any for the sad tooth-lessness of the 34-year-old Charlotte Brontë. No woman, said George Smith (sympathetically), wanted more to be pretty. The blue pill did not help.

TRANSFORMATION

The central crux in *Wuthering Heights* occurs when Heathcliff overhears Cathy say, in conversation with Nelly, 'It would degrade me to marry Heathcliff now.' It's an odd scene. Nelly is 'sensible of Heathcliff's presence' – she knows he is eavesdropping. But she does not, as a well-intentioned person would, warn Cathy, who is unaware Heathcliff is listening. It looks suspiciously as if Nelly leads Cathy on.

Heathcliff does not linger to hear anything more than that awful word 'degrade'. He runs off, taking nothing with him (money?) and leaving no explanation, verbal or written. He van-ishes and remains vanished. He leaves Wuthering Heights in August 1780. Over the next three years there are no letters, nor any other news about him.

Jump to September 1783. Cathy has married the un-degrading Edgar. Nelly too has come up in the world. She is now housekeeper at the Lintons' Thrushcross Grange. A top spot. 'Nelly' is now 'Mrs Dean' (the title is honorary, not marital). Was this why she connived to get Heathcliff out of the way (see below, 'Villainy', page 180)?

It is 'mellow' evening. Nelly has been picking apples. Dusk is falling, the moon is rising. Then, out of the shadows, from nowhere:

I heard a voice behind me say –

'Nelly, is that you?'

It was a deep voice, and foreign in tone; yet there was something in the manner of pronouncing my name which made it sound familiar.

The word 'foreign' is arresting. Nelly turns to make out, in the shadows, 'a tall man dressed in dark clothes, with dark face and hair'. She still does not recognise him. 'Look, I'm not a stranger!' the dark man tells her:

A ray fell on his features; the cheeks were sallow, and half covered with black whiskers; the brows lowering, the eyes deep set and singular. I remembered the eyes.

Full recognition is hampered by the fact that he seems a different man from the stable boy who ran away three years ago. 'And you are Heathcliff!' Nelly finally says, adding, 'But altered! Nay, there's no comprehending it. Have you been for a soldier?'

He does not answer the question. When informed by Nelly that Heathcliff is back, and wishes to see his wife, Edgar insultingly asks, 'What, the gipsy – the plough-boy?' But the visitor no longer occupies that lowly position in life. Nelly immediately apprehends that she must address him, henceforth, as 'Mr Heathcliff'.

Mr Heathcliff has money in his pocket – funds enough to gamble for high stakes with the drunken Hindley and win, over the table, possession of Wuthering Heights. How has the 'transformation of Heathcliff', as Nelly calls it, happened?

Looking at his 'athletic' frame and his upright stance, she

continues to suppose he has been in the army. The American War of Independence was still raging in the early 1780s. But taking the king's shilling and serving in the lowest ranks, would not have transformed the ploughboy into a gentleman.

His face, when Nelly can study it in the light,

> looked intelligent, and retained no marks of former degradation. A half-civilised ferocity lurked yet in the depressed brows and eyes full of black fire, but it was subdued; and his manner was even dignified: quite divested of roughness …

Only the black fire in the eyes recalls the old 'untransformed' Heathcliff.

Is Nelly's supposition, that he joined the army, plausible if we assume that Corporal Heathcliff became an officer's servant (like Thackeray's Barry Lyndon, a novel the Brontës may have read in its *Fraser's Magazine* serialisation) and learned, by observation of the officer class, social graces, and how to shave and dress himself elegantly? But how, if that were the case, did he get all his money? Theft? Gambling? (where did he learn to play the gentleman's game, picquet, so well?)

A flight of fantasy could explain the transformation. Heathcliff has spent three years at university – abroad, perhaps (recall the foreign accent). Patrick Brontë had left Ireland, a son of the soil, and in three years he was a young Cantab, a gentleman, with a foreign (English) accent and prospects.

Alas, the undergraduate Heathcliff is not a convincing fable. One dismisses it out of hand. What, then? It has been convincingly argued that the Brontës read Bulwer Lytton and that *Wuthering Heights* contains echoes of Lytton's then-popular (now jeered at)* fiction. Has Heathcliff, like Paul Clifford in the 'Newgate novel' of that title, taken the night road as a gentleman highwayman?

Did he, perhaps, take off somewhere and set himself up as a gigolo seducer of rich women, trading on his good looks, burning eyes, ruthlessness and white teeth (see above, 'Toothsome', page 165)?

A little thought on the matter, if one must come up with an explanation, suggests that he returned to where he started in life: Liverpool. By the mid-18th century the city had overtaken London and Bristol in the exportation of slaves, in the golden triangle between Africa, Britain, and the West Indies. For a man of Heathcliff's intelligent savagery and moral unscrupulosity the opportunities in Liverpool would be immense.

However the 'transformation' happened, neither Heathcliff, nor the novel, give the slightest explanation. It leaves a question every reader must, after a careful reading, decide for themselves.

There is an additional question. Is this black hole at the centre of Brontë's narrative artistic design? Aesthetic vacancy? Heathcliff, from his origin onwards, pulsates darkness. Is that the motive? Or is it simply that Emily Brontë, country mouse that she was, did not know enough of the outside world to invent a convincing storyline? Literary critical judgement has come down strongly in favour of the first. So do I. The narrative darkness around Heathcliff is as artful as a Whistler nocturne.

* See the annual 'dark and stormy night' competition for opening lines as bad as that of *Paul Clifford* (1830).

VAMPIROLOGY (1)

"'Is he a ghoul, or a vampire?' I mused. I had read of such hideous incarnate demons.' Nelly is wondering about Heathcliff in his last night as a living being on earth.

Ghouls (*ghūls*) Nelly could plausibly have read about in some version of the *Arabian Nights*. But where, one may ask, did Mistress Ellen Dean read about vampires? Heathcliff, one recalls, kills himself in April 1802, by the novel's timeline.

There is an oblique reference to vampirism in Robert Southey's twelve-book epic *Thalaba the Destroyer* – although it's hard to imagine Nelly wading through the puddingy mass. The Brontës may have read it, before sending off their poems to the poet laureate. The first popularisation of the subject of vampirism came with Lord Byron's bestselling oriental romance *The Giaour*, which came out in 1813. Viz. the curse:

> But first, on earth as vampire sent,
> Thy corpse shall from its tomb be rent:
> Then ghostly haunt thy native place,
> And suck the blood of all thy race;

Vampires, as a superstition, are as old as mankind's decision to dispose, decently, of its dead mankind.* It took literature a long time to realise what a rich vein they could open.

Nelly's reference is an anachronism, but an interesting one. It tells us something about her but also rather more

---

* See the classic work on the subject, Paul Barber, *Vampires, Burial and Death* (1988).

about the Brontës. The children were all Byronists, from the creation of Glasstown onwards. It's safe to guess they knew *The Giaour*.

It is possible, of course, that Emily Brontë had got wind of the bestseller which was taking off serially as she was writing *Wuthering Heights*: James Rymer's *Varney the Vampire*. But it's crude stuff, originating in the depths of penny literature and sub-Gothic spine-chillers for the semi-literate masses. The classic works of vampire literature, *Carmilla* and *Dracula*, would not appear until decades after all the Brontës had gone to their rest, their line extinct.

If not *The Giaour* or *Varney the Vampire*, Emily's principal source (which may, indirectly, have had some formative effect on the creation of Heathcliff) can almost certainly be traced back to the legendarily wet summer of 1816. The downpours prevented a party of distinguished literary tourists in Switzerland – Lord Byron, Percy Shelley, Mary Godwin, Claire Clairmont and John Polidori – from actually touring. They were confined to their rented accommodation. And very bored.

The bad weather had begun, far away, in Indonesia, with the eruption of Mount Tambora. It hit seven on the Volcanic Explosivity Index, making it a thousand-year event. The result, worldwide, was the 'year without a summer' and, concurrently, a remarkable eruption of Gothicism in Villa Diodati, alongside Lake Geneva, where the English tourists were staying.

Pent up by the foul weather, they beguiled the rainy days and nights with light reading and a competition to write the most spine-chilling ghost story their *ennuyés* minds could come up with. Mary Godwin (soon to be Mary Shelley) elected to rewrite *Paradise Lost* as *Frankenstein*. Shelley and Byron rather fizzled out: literature was more than a parlour game for them.

The author of 'The Vampyre', 'Dr' Polidori was a graduate of Edinburgh medical school. Polidori had learned his sawbone trade on cadavers criminally supplied by Edinburgh's 'resurrectionists'. Burke and Hare were the most notorious practitioners of that grisly trade. (Heathcliff, of course, is also a resurrectionist.) Byron had recruited 'Polly' for the duration of the tour abroad, on a handsome stipend of £500.

The plot of 'The Vampyre' is simple. The sinister Lord Ruthven takes the handsome young Aubrey on a Continental tour with him. On his travels, Ruthven cold-bloodedly destroys every young person who comes his way. Finally, having sucked Aubrey dry as a walnut shell, he turns his dead, grey, irresistible eye on Aubrey's sister:

> The guardians hastened to protect Miss Aubrey; but when they arrived, it was too late. Lord Ruthven had disappeared, and Aubrey's sister had glutted the thirst of a VAMPYRE!

Ruthven was conceived as an idoliser's compliment to Byron the irresistible.

Byron had soon had more of the young man than he could stand and sent him on his way to cross the Alps, alone, friendless and penniless. 'The Vampyre' was long forgotten until it rose from the grave in suspicious circumstances. Henry Colburn, the most unscrupulous publisher in London, put it out in 1819 as 'by Lord Byron'. Polidori protested bitterly, and in vain. Money talked. With Byron's name attached to it, 'the trashy tale' was sensationally popular. Polidori profited not at all. He died aged 25, suicidally depressed and probably by a self-administered dose of prussic acid. But it's a safe bet his little book planted a seed at Haworth. And an interesting anachronism in *Wuthering Heights*.

VAMPIROLOGY (2)

There is another curious reference to the undead in *Jane Eyre*. 'Shall I tell you of what it reminded me?' the heroine asks Rochester, having seen his wife. 'You may,' he graciously replies. Not a 'madwoman', she says. Bertha reminds her 'of the foul German spectre – the Vampyre'. Jane is recalling an older tradition of the female vampire – something virtually obliterated in contemporary folklore. These female vampires were purple in hue, full of blood – it was their victims who were cadaverous. The description fits Bertha, to a 'v', one is tempted to say.

> The maniac bellowed: she parted her shaggy locks from her visage, and gazed wildly at her visitors. I recognised well that purple face,—those bloated features.

Her sharp teeth sink, thirstily, into Rochester's cheek. Blood drips down her chin.

The pale, famished, rather dapper vampire of today's screen, a later variation, was originated by Bram Stoker. He is conventionally male. The Draculas, and sub-Draculas may, of course, have had a harem of toothsome living-dead lovelies in attendance but vampirism, since Stoker, has been seen as essentially manly.

Charlotte, I suspect, was, in inventing Rochester's Jamaican bride, thinking of Goethe's well-known poem, 'The Bride of Corinth'. It centres on an undead woman who rises from the grave to revenge herself on a faithless 'spouse':

Nightly from my narrow chamber driven,
Come I to fulfil my destin'd part,
Him to seek to whom my troth was given,
And to draw the life-blood from his heart.

Marriage and vampirism are symbolically conjoined, as erotic blood-union. The victim wife becomes murderess. There is no actual use of the V-word in Goethe's poem. But the vindictive exsanguination says it all. 'The Bride of Corinth' is called, popularly, 'the first vampire poem', and it's odds-on Charlotte wants us to know Jane Eyre has read it.

VEGETARIANISM

Mrs Gaskell got her most colourful details about everyday life at Haworth in the 1820s from a dubious source. Subsequent biographers have lined up for and against what Mrs Martha Wright 'revealed'. Or maliciously 'invented' (see above, 'Normality?', page 113). Martha was a local nurse, employed by the Brontës when they came to Haworth. She attended Patrick's wife as she died, from cancer, in 1821. It was an unsettled period for the family. Wright was subsequently dismissed by Patrick – a Grace Poole-like weakness for the bottle is sometimes surmised. Nonetheless, she survived the whole family and was a wholly respectable woman when Gaskell interviewed her.* She may, however, have had a burning grudge, nursed for thirty years.

* See Ann Dinsdale, 'Mrs Brontë's Nurse', Brontë Studies (November 2005).

Patrick

It was Wright who revealed/invented the image of a Revd Brontë who would cut up his wife's and daughters' clothes and shoes, if they were, to his mind, irreligiously colourful, and who would blaze away with his pistol around the church and parsonage grounds like a western cowboy on a Saturday night. A broad streak of madness was hinted at. Mrs Gaskell swallowed it all.

The following, however, is one of the more curious facts Martha passed on:

there never were such good children. I used to think them spiritless, they were so different to any children I had ever seen. In part, I set it down to a fancy Mr. Brontë had of not letting them have flesh-meat to eat. It was from no wish for saving, for there was plenty and even waste in the house, with young servants and no mistress to see after them; but he thought that children should be brought up simply and hardily: so they had nothing but potatoes for their dinner; but they never seemed to wish for anything else; they were good little creatures.

This 'fact', when Gaskell put it into print, was objected to by Patrick. Evidence, from servants and the local butcher, was dug up to contradict the Wright/Gaskell allegation of vegetarian tyrannies at the parsonage. The contradictions are persuasive.

It's an interesting canard, however, and bears a little examination. Patrick was an intellectual – Cambridge had left that mark on him. And, we can safely surmise, he was interested in the various energies and ideas coursing through the branch of evangelical Anglicanism he had affiliated himself to.

Forty miles away, in Manchester – workshop of the world – one of the most innovative breakaway movements was introduced by William Cowherd (1763–1816), with his 'Bible Christians'.

Spiritually restless, Cowherd – originally a Swedenborgian – set up his own chapel in Salford in 1809, splitting from the Church of England in which he had been ordained. Cowherdism took, as its main tenet, vegetarianism. Congregants were not admitted unless they had abstained from meat for three months.

Cowherd believed it was God's will that man not eat animal flesh (otherwise, he suggested, it would grow on trees, or in the ground). Adam and Eve were vegetarians, until they sinned. Cowherdism was an extension of the temperance movement and the larger moral reforms brought in by ultra-evangelical enthusiasm. Abstinence from meat lowered aggression and temptations to other dissipations. Meatlessness was next to Godliness.

Cowherd set up a medical centre and a library and distributed vegetable soup to the distressed classes of Manchester. Despite Lancashire's love of meat ('hot-pot', 'tripe and onions', etc.), Cowherd's Christian vegetarianism took off. More vegetarian eateries were set up in Manchester than in any other city. He and his 'Cowherdite' disciple the Revd Joseph Brotherton are seen as the founders of what became, in 1847, the British Vegetarian Society, and of (via Brotherton) the early vegetarian movements in the US.

All this was happening in Haworth's vicinity. Clergymen would certainly have been aware of what one of their most enterprising brethren was doing. What one can plausibly surmise is that Patrick was sufficiently curious to at least think about curbing the exuberance of his offspring (and possibly himself) by meatlessness. He may even have wondered if it was the religious thing to do.

Whatever was served on the table, and in what amount, the idea of vegetarianism was in the air at Haworth Parsonage. To that degree, Martha Wright's testimony can be believed.

VILLAINY

Notwithstanding that there are those who see something heroic in Heathcliff, to ask who the villain is in *Wuthering Heights* seems equivalent to asking who is the bad guy in whatever James Bond volume, from Le Chiffre onwards. Nonetheless, greater works of literature than Ian Fleming's have inner enigmas as to moral judgement, or who should wear the black hat. It's what the greatest of 20th-century literary critics, Frank Kermode, called those works 'patience'. They throw back different answers at different times and to different generations of reader.

Every generation of critics, for example (often in open, Oedipal rebellion against the previous 'paternal' generation), interprets Shakespeare differently. Sometimes radically so. Who is more in the right? Samuel Johnson or Professor James S. Shapiro (winner of the 2006 Samuel Johnson Prize for Non-Fiction).*

For those who lived through the 1950s and early 1960s, those decades were the era of what was called 'deep reading'. Irony was uncovered everywhere. Great literature was conceived of as a casket, or a safe: you 'cracked' it, and found, secreted inside, the unexpected meaning. Eureka!

A kind of ingenious perversity ruled. The villain in Hamlet? Hamlet. Don't ask. The founding example was Edmund Wilson's reading of Henry James's *The Turn of the Screw*. There were no ghosts: it was all a fantasy of the governess. The villain of the piece wasn't Quint (a distant descendant, one might think, of villainous Heathcliff) but the deranged 'guardian'. She, it was, who corrupted and killed poor little Miles.

As regards *Wuthering Heights*, deep reading reached its most profound – some would say absurd – in James Hafley's 1958 article in *Nineteenth-Century Fiction* (the voice of critical authority in the field). Hafley unmasked Nelly Dean as 'one of the consummate villains in English literature': a veritable 'Iago' in the kitchen.

The thesis runs against the grain of the novel, as it appears on the surface; but, once you open the mind, an argument can be posed. Nelly's first appearance in the drama is as a mother figure, 'nursing' Lockwood. We can almost imagine her spooning her

* For *1599: A Year in the Life of William Shakespeare*.

medicinal soups into her employer's lips and telling him a bed-time story about high drama at Wuthering Heights, the house which has terrified and almost killed him. Nelly's name itself throws back a warm echo.*

But is Nelly Dean, via whom the bulk of the story is delivered, that elusive thing, 'a reliable narrator'? And the other narrators: Zillah; Isabella, in her letter, retailing the facts about the Heathcliff she discovered after marriage? Are they reliable?

Is Lockwood, even, that stupid, shallow man, reliable. And, if trustworthy, are these eyewitnesses who mediate the text, conveying it and quite plausibly blurring it, perceptive enough to understand (as the 'deep reader' can) what their eyes witness? Do they have distorting interests of their own which distort and obscure?

The casting of Nelly as the black hat in the novel pivots on something that runs against common sense (as does the casting of Bertha Mason as the heroine of *Jane Eyre* – see above, 'Attic Matters', page 6) – namely that the novel was universally misread until, 110 years later, an enlightened generation of readers happened to come along and look at it the right, topsy-turvy way.

Overlooking that unconvincing fact, so unflattering to what Samuel Johnson and Virginia Woolf called (approvingly) the 'common reader', what is the evidence? First is the fact we know nothing about Nelly's origins, other than that her mother (since deceased) was wet nurse to the Earnshaw children. Her father? Unknown. She is, perhaps, illegitimate. Was she one of Earnshaw Snr's by-blows (as it is sometimes suggested Heathcliff is)?

---

* Originating in folk music, the name evokes what became a popular music hall song: 'There's an old mill by the stream, Nellie Dean/Where we used to sit and dream, Nellie Dean'.

Nelly is impressively literate (see above, 'Vampirology [1]', page 173). She is not, like the other two named servants in the house, Joseph and Zillah, Methodistical, but, we deduce Anglican – one of the Gimmerton Kirk congregation. It was the kirk's Sunday School which, perhaps, educated her. That and books she found lying about, and in the Grange's well-stocked library.

She has a forename and surname, unlike the other servants, indicating hierarchical superiority in the domestic world. And she has a career. Nelly is, in time, a housekeeper at Thrushcross Grange. A senior position, earning her the honorific title 'Mrs Dean' (what Lockwood calls her). It's a courtesy title. There is no evidence Nelly has a husband, or children; nor do we know of any romantic interest in her early years.

There is one convincing piece of evidence for the 'consummate villain' thesis. When the young Heathcliff is brought back, hissing like a demon child, it is Nelly who takes the initiative. Hindley and Catherine will have nothing to do with their new, adoptive, sibling. They refuse to share their bed with 'it'. Or even have 'it' in their room. 'I,' Nelly tells Lockwood,

> had no more sense, so I put it on the landing of the stairs, hoping it might be gone on the morrow. By chance, or else attracted by hearing his voice, it crept to Mr. Earnshaw's door, and there he found it on quitting his chamber. Inquiries were made as to how it got there; I was obliged to confess, and in recompense for my cowardice and inhumanity was sent out of the house.

When she returns she is not a quasi-daughter of the household, but a servant. This demotion, it is suggested, explains her decades' long revenge.

There are throwaway remarks, which may be thought to support this reading. 'Hindley hated [Heathcliff],' she says, 'and to say the truth I did the same.' Nelly has complicated feelings – apparently jealous feelings – about Cathy, her infant equal (did they not suck at the same breast?), now her mistress:

> She [Cathy] did turn out a haughty, headstrong creature! I own I did not like her, after infancy was past; and I vexed her frequently by trying to bring down her arrogance: she never took an aversion to me, though.

Social demotion is a regular event at Wuthering Heights. When he inherits, Hindley demotes Heathcliff from a son of the house to the lowly status of a 'groom'. A stable boy. Heathcliff, in turn, demotes the bloodline son of the house, Hareton, to the condition of a loutish peasant. He takes pleasure in the degradation. These ups and downs are serious matters.

Hafley and other sharp-eyed readers pick up on such things as Nelly's withholding the fact that Cathy, her mistress, is at death's door. 'I kept it to myself,' she says, ensuring that her mistress goes through the door all the quicker. Cathy, on her part, comes out with the accusation 'Nelly is my hidden enemy'. Hidden no more.

But is she (a 'consummate villain', that is)? There is a moment in the action in which Nelly reflects on her actions. This is a key piece of evidence – a *mea culpa* almost – in the prosecution case:

> I seated myself in a chair, and rocked to and fro, passing harsh judgment on my many derelictions of duty; from which, it struck me then, all the misfortunes of my employers sprang. It was not the case, in reality, I am

aware; but it was, in my imagination, that dismal night; and I thought Heathcliff himself less guilty than I.

The 1950s are long gone. But contemporary readers may find a quaint pleasure in rereading Hafley, with its 'Ha! I have you now, you dastardly housekeeper; you didn't think you could throw the dust in the reader's eyes forever, did you, you consummate villain!'.

WHITHER WUTHER?

Ask yourself: have you ever heard anyone use the term 'wuthering', other than in reference to Emily Brontë's novel?

Would a TV weather forecaster, for example warn us about 'wuthering winds coming in with a low pressure system building up over the West Riding of Yorkshire'?

The *Oxford English Dictionary*, that normally omniscient fount of etymology, semantics and usage, is in a rare state of bamboozlement about the word. It can't find, honestly, any usage of the verb 'to wuther', and its present participle anywhere in the deepest recesses of the English language. The entry founders in the quagmire of Middle English, e.g.:

Forms: ME **quhedir, quhethir, qwedyr,** ME–15 **quhidder,** 15 **quhiddir.**

It's not terribly enlightening. Even less so is our reminding of the Old Norse **hviðra* '(compare Norwegian *kvidra*)'. There are also some dubious Scotticisms cited (to 'whudder', for example).

To be honest, the first genuine usage the dictionary can find is Emily's and the best definition Lockwood's (as much a stranger to the word as us, the readers):

Wuthering Heights is the name of Mr. Heathcliff's dwelling. 'Wuthering' being a significant provincial adjective, descriptive of the atmospheric tumult to which its station is exposed, in stormy weather.

I have a strong suspicion that Emily made it up. Wuthering Heights. It's as much a confection as Edmund Lear's great Gromboolian plain. I expect a torrent of email from the West Riding putting me right on the matter.

What is odd, however, is that having been put into current knowledge so spectacularly, no one uses it in everyday speech. It is Emily Brontë's word, and hers alone.

WINDOWS

I've lived professionally with articles in learned journals for 60 years – consuming and producing them *en masse*. Relatively few of mine or anyone else's have had lasting effect: most are scholarly noise, proof of scholarly life, like the mist on the mirror held to the lips of a dead-or-alive person. Hum of the academic hive.

As regards the Brontës, a genuinely thought-changing article was published in *Nineteenth-Century Fiction* (December 1952), a premier journal, by a scholar of less than (then) premier eminence. Dorothy Van Ghent published relatively little during her, sadly short, career. Van Ghent's criticism, gathered into monograph, drily entitled *The English Novel: Form and Function*, in 1953, is a high point of what was called 'New Criticism' in the US, 'Practical Criticism' in the UK, and 'close reading' by those not in the academic world. It amounted to picking up and shaking the text vigorously to see what meanings would drop out.

Van Ghent's seminal *NCF* article was called, again drily, 'The Window Figure and the Two Children Figure in *Wuthering Heights*'. Ask what is the most disturbing scene in the Brontës' fiction, said Van Ghent (uncontroversially, I suspect), and it would be the ghost scene at the beginning of *Wuthering Heights*. Lockwood has been put to bed, by Zillah's mistake, in Cathy's old room – her shrine, as Heathcliff regards it, awaiting her return from the other side.

The bed, coffin-like in its curtained compactness, is one of the old-fashioned 'closet' variety, joined as a fixture to the window wall (God knows how Zillah tucked the sheets in). After a bed-time reading of the sermons of Jabes Branderham, Lockwood falls into troubled slumber and, eventually, full-blown nightmare. A spectral figure wakes him, scratching at the window pane, inches from his face and the now guttered-out candle. Moonlight. He opens the latched window reaches through and holds the thing's ('its') frozen paw:

> 'Who are you?' I asked, struggling, meanwhile, to dis-engage myself. 'Catherine Linton,' it replied, shiveringly (why did I think of Linton? I had read Earnshaw twenty times for Linton). 'I'm come home: I'd lost my way on the moor!'
>
> As it spoke, I discerned, obscurely, a child's face look-ing through the window. Terror made me cruel; and, finding it useless to attempt shaking the creature off, I

pulled its wrist on to the broken pane, and rubbed it
to and fro till the blood ran down and soaked the bed-
clothes; still it wailed, 'Let me in!' and maintained its
tenacious grip, almost maddening me with fear.

In modern times Emily could challenge Stephen King as a
writer of horror. Who knows if her lost second novel developed
that genre.

That Lockwood (the name, etymologically, means 'close the
door', 'keep it out') should commit this act of gratuitous violence,
scraping a little girl's wrists on jagged glass, is as horrific as it is
out of character.

Van Ghent reminds us, this is the swinging open and shut
window at which, a couple of years on, Heathcliff, reaching *his*
hand into the world outside, will die. The crucial point, Van
Ghent argues, is that this scene, along with four other key scenes
in the novel, is centred on the metaphor – the *topos* – of the
window.

Window glass is the transparent membrane between oppos-
ing realities: between the dream world and the outer world;
between the domestic 'real' world and the terrifying alien world
of the external 'other'. It is materially there and not there.* The
window lets vision through, but obstructs physical passage. All
the Brontës, it's worth remembering, were acutely short-sighted
and saw the world through glass. If, that is, they wanted to see
the world clearly.

---

* Mirror glass is as rich metaphorically, but differently so: it reverses
reality. Lewis Carroll plays with the idea in Alice's expedition through
the looking-glass.

The window's second significant entry into the novel comes when the young savages Heathcliff and Catherine, peeping Toms both of them, wonder at the civilised world of the Lintons at Thrushcross Grange: 'a splendid place carpeted with crimson'. Heathcliff rejects what he sees through the window; Catherine is seduced and is 'taken in', in both senses. She goes through the window.

The third window scene has Catherine at death's door (or death's window), trying to escape through the obstructing glass (now imprisoning her) back to the moors, Wuthering Heights and Heathcliff. Defying Nelly and her doctors – not to mention common sense – she throws open the window to the cold air outside, hastening her death and (what she wants) re-entry into the wild 'other' world outside. If death is required to get there, so be it.

And, of course, Heathcliff 'catches his death' at a window at the conclusion of the novel. Much of the power of this most powerful novel is contained in the 'window figure', Van Ghent argues. Convincingly. My copy of *The English Novel: Form and Function*, which I read as an undergraduate, is black with marginal comment.

My academic generation had, soon after, to learn new tricks. 'New Criticism' was old hat by the 1970s. 'Theory' (an offshoot of French philosophy) had replaced it as the interpretative vehicle of choice for younger scholars. But it is pleasant to note that the classic text of the newer, theoretical, criticism, Roland Barthes' *S/Z*, which broke down narrative into its five intermingled 'codes', has an interesting resemblance to Van Ghent's old-hat close reading.

Barthes' study, with a group of his like-mindedly clever postgraduates, dismembers Balzac's short story *Sarassine*. It opens:

I was buried in one of those profound reveries to which
everybody, even a frivolous man, is subject in the midst
of the most uproarious festivities. The clock on the
Elysée-Bourbon had just struck midnight. Seated in
a window recess and concealed behind the undulating
folds of a curtain of watered silk, I was able to contem-
plate at my leisure the garden of the mansion at which I
was passing the evening. The trees, being partly covered
with snow, were outlined indistinctly against the gray-
ish background formed by a cloudy sky, barely whitened
by the moon. Seen through the medium of that strange
atmosphere, they bore a vague resemblance to spectres
carelessly enveloped in their shrouds, a gigantic image of
the famous *Dance of Death*. Then, turning in the other
direction, I could gaze admiringly upon the dance of the
living! a magnificent salon, with walls of silver and gold,
with gleaming chandeliers, and bright with the light of
many candles.

The central character, Sarassine, owns two sexual realities:
the reader (and narrator) believe her a beautiful woman. In a
stroke-of-thunder denouement she/he is revealed to be something other. Barthes makes much of the window, and the opening
scene, as a prime example of the 'metaphorical' code, and the par-
adoxes it embodies.

Dorothy Van Ghent, had she lived to read *S/Z*, would have
been justified in chortling. 'Go figure,' she might have said.

APPENDIX

Jane Eyre abbreviated

by John Crace

John Crace is the parliamentary sketch writer for the Guardian *newspaper, for which he also writes the regular Digested Read feature. He is the author of several books including, with John Sutherland, the multi-volume* The Incomplete Shakespeare.

'You are not a pleasant girl,' said my aunt, Mrs Reed. 'You have been found being beastly to my dear son, John. You are to be locked in the red-room.'

Reader, how I longed to say that it was John who had bullied me, not I him! But in truth I was beside myself; or, as the French say, out of myself. Why was I always suffering, always browbeaten, forever condemned? I had not asked to be an orphan nor to be lodged with my aunt.

As day turned to night, a dark terror enveloped me and I did sense the ghost of my dead uncle pass before me. My head spun wildly and I did scream but to no avail and ere long I fell unconscious in gothic terror. It was not until the following morning that I was released and summoned before my aunt.

'You are still a very unpleasant girl,' my aunt observed.

'And you are a very unpleasant woman,' I replied with unexpected boldness for a ten-year-old girl.

'Enough, I say. It is time you were taught some manners. Henceforward you are to go to Lowood school to be taught some manners by Mr Brocklehurst.'

Lowood school, how aptly named it was. For seldom had I felt so low as when I arrived at that institution.

'You are a mean and unpleasant girl,' said Mr Brocklehurst, forcing me to stand upon a chair in front of the entire school of wretched, impoverished orphans. 'You shall remain standing until you learn some manners. Only then will you be allowed a bowl of gruel.'

'But sir, I am just a proto-feminist who likes to speak her mind,' I replied.

'There, there,' said the matron, the kindly Miss Temple – truly my life was blessed with nominative determinism for Miss Temple was to become my Miss Sanctuary – as she put me to bed. 'You may be very plain, plain Jane, and your teeth might also be in a hell of a state, just like Miss Brontë's, but I don't think you are intrinsically evil. Just try not to rub too many people up the wrong way.'

That night, I heard a coughing in the dormitory.

'I am dying of consumption,' said an enfeebled Helen Burns. 'But do not cry for me, because I am stoical unto death and accepting of my role within this book to be the voice of martyred innocence.'

Reader, I know I am defective in many areas of my character – false modesty being one of them – but I never tired of spending time with Helen Burns. Mainly because she died almost immediately thereafter. But reader, let it be known that never a day went past for the rest of my life when I did not think upon her with affection even though I was never to mention her again.

Hitherto I have recorded in some detail the events of the first ten years of my insignificant existence, but of the next eight I have little to say other than that I found myself unexpectedly happy – a state of affairs that served no purpose to my narrative. And so it was that in my eighteenth year, I found myself journeying to Thornfield – how aptly named again, for my adventures there were to be most thorny – where I was to take up a position as governess to Adèle, a young French girl who was ward of a Mr Rochester.

'Bonjour plain Jane,' said Adèle. 'Avez-vous come ici to teach me Franglais?'

'Bien sur,' I replied. 'But moins of the plain Jane. I've got everyone else telling me I'm not beaucoup of a looker without vous wading dans.'

The days passed easily enough, though I did once or twice imagine I heard the sound of a vampyre in the attic, and it wasn't until some months later that I finally met Mr Rochester. Reader, it happened like this. I was out walking late one night, when I heard a horse galloping along the lane followed by the cry of a man.

'You spooked the horse and made him slip,' said the man.

'Don't you start blaming me for things before we've even met,' I said. 'People have been doing that to me all my life.'

'You must be Janet,' he said.

'Jane,' I replied.

'That's what I said. Now, Janet you must walk with me and tell me how young Adèle is shaping up.'

Over the following weeks we had many such conversations and I fancy Mr Rochester came to appreciate my northern bluntness. 'Plain by name and plain by nature,' he used to say teasingly. Reader, I hesitate to say this but I began to find a certain attractiveness in Mr Rochester's high forehead and haughty demeanour, but being so plain I never once imagined those feelings to be reciprocated. Even when I rescued him from a fire in his bedroom, the cause of which he never did satisfactorily explain.

'Tell me, Janet,' he said, some days later.

'It's Jane.'

'Tell me, Janet. What do you think of Miss Blanche Ingram? Do you not think she is a fine specimen of woman and would make a good wife.'

I had had reason to observe Miss Ingram and Mr Rochester closely for some weeks and could only agree that she was indeed tall, comely and in possession of most of her teeth.

'That settles it, Janet,' he declared. 'I shall be wed. Will you still love me?'

'I'm sure you'll be very happy,' I replied, struggling to repress my turbulent emotions.

'Then *we* shall be wed,' he bellowed. 'I was only pretending to love Blanche to see if you really loved me. For at heart, I am a deeply insecure man with extreme trust issues.'

Reader, forgive me. I know I am meant to be a feminist role model and that I ought to have told him to get stuffed if he thought I was going to get married to someone who could play such abusive mind games. But reader, I am plain and I was unlikely to get a better offer. Besides, I did really fancy him and it wasn't his fault that he had had such a tortured life and he could be quite nice when he tried.

To my surprise, his family were greatly pleased by our betrothal and the weeks before we were to be wed passed agreeably while preparations were made, though it was quite annoying to one day find my wedding dress had been ripped in half.

'It's those ghosts, Janet …'

'Jane ...'

'They get everywhere round here. Never mind, I'll get you another.'

Reader, imagine my excitement on the big day when the clergyman asked Edward if he would agree to take me, Janet, as his lawful wedded wife. Reader, imagine my horror when a breathless solicitor turned up at the church and announced that the wedding could not go ahead as he was already married.

'I'm really sorry,' said Edward. 'I was going to tell you, but it just completely slipped my mind. It's like this. I was very young and when my parents told me to get married to this rich creole woman, Bertha, I did as I was told. Only it turned out she was mad; it's possible she even has syphilis and has given it to me. Anyway, I was then so distraught to be with a madwoman that I went to France where I had an affair with Adèle's mother – though I swear on my life I wasn't the dad – and when she dumped me I shagged several other women before coming back to ——shire.'

'Oh Edward, we all make mistakes,' I said; despite all I had heard, I loved him still.

'Thank you, plain Janet. I knew you'd understand.'

We took the coach back to Thornfield, there to be greeted by a huge, dark, deranged woman.

'Ah, that's the other thing I forgot to tell you. Bertha's been living upstairs all along. It wasn't ghosts you were hearing, it was her.'

'Nnnnnng,' grunted Bertha.

'Such a pity Miss Brontë hasn't allowed her a single word in the entire novel,' said Edward. 'Still, I'm sure she would have corroborated every detail of my story, Wouldn't you, Bertha?'

'Nnnnnng.'

'Now plain Janet,' Edward continued. 'That just leaves us to decide what to do next, now we can't get married. Here's what I propose. You come with me and live as my mistress in Marseille and I'll do my best not to give you syphilis.'

'Mr Rochester,' I said, drawing myself up to my full four feet six inches. 'I may be very plain, but I do have some self-worth. I will not be your mistress.'

'Oh go on.'

'No.'

With that I collected my possessions and took a coach as far as my last remaining sovereign would take me. Reader, a storm it blowed hard and I would certainly have died that night had I not been taken in by the two Miss Rivers of Moor House, which was, not surprisingly, on a moor.

Reader, how my heart flowed with gratitude to the two Miss Rivers and how pleased they were to discover that I was able to converse easily in French while drawing a perfect likeness of them both.

'Now we know you are a lady fallen on hard times and not some penniless scrounger,' they said in unison, 'we are happy to let you stay with us for as long as you wish and to meet our brother St John, the local clergyman.'

'I would not want to be beholden to you,' I said. 'I will earn my keep.'

'In that case, you can be the headmistress of the local school for girls,' said St John, not unthoughtfully.

Reader, I loved that job and worked hard to educate the poor, and I must confess it was a complete surprise when I found out that not only had I inherited £20,000 from uncle John, but that St John and his sisters were my cousins. Who would have imagined such a thing?

'Happily will I divide my fortune with you three,' I told my cousins.

'We don't mind if you do,' they said.

Some months later St John took me to one side.

'I wish you to be my wife, learn Hindustani and travel with me among the natives spreading the word of God.'

'Sir,' I replied, 'Much as I too like God, I'm not sure I much care for your disapproving Calvinist manner and I'm certain you don't love me because you regard me with such icy stares.'

'You must marry me.'

'I will not. Though I will travel to India as your cousin.'

'That's not good enough,' he said, in a decidedly ungodly tone.

Reader, just then a vision of Mr Rochester came upon me, calling me to his side so I packed my possessions and headed off back across the moor. My heart shook with terror when I espied Thornfield once more, for the house was but a burnt-out ruin.

I quickened my pace and there he was, sitting under a tree, armless and eyeless.

'Is that you, plain Janet?' he enquired.

'It's Jane.'

'It is you, Janet. I know not what to say. Mad Bertha did set the house alight and I was sorely injured while trying to rescue her.'

'And what of mad Bertha?'

'She slipped from the battlements. I swear I did not push her.'

'Then thou art redeemed, for God has now punished you enough for all your porkies. Since thou art blind it does not really matter how plain I am. And happily will I be thy right hand.'

'Now you're talking.'

'Enough of that.'

Reader, I married him. And as the years passed, so some sight returned to his eyes and he did finally get to see our firstborn son. Though he, like me, could not for the life of him remember what he was called.

Postscript by John Sutherland

John Crace is right about 'Janet Eyre': Rochester calls her by this name on a number of occasions. The wobbly forename is usually explained thus: (1) it was a common term of endearment for women called 'Jane'; (2) Rochester is a lover of all things French (particularly French women) and it is a casual anglicisation of 'Jeanette'.